THE AI PLAYBOOK FOR BEGINNERS

MASTER THE FUNDAMENTALS OF GENERATIVE AI, CHATGPT & MACHINE LEARNING TO 10X PRODUCTIVITY, ENHANCE CREATIVITY AND OPTIMIZE EVERYDAY LIFE

KAI SINCLAIR

CONTENTS

INTRODUCTION

Ever wonder how your favorite coffee shop knows just when to brew your morning latte or how your playlist seems to read your mind? Meet Alex, a graphic designer by day and an AI enthusiast by night. Every morning, Alex's AI assistant syncs with their calendar, suggests the best route to work, and even crafts an email response for that tricky client. In the evening, it curates a playlist that matches Alex's mood, winding down the day with the perfect soundtrack. This isn't science fiction—it's the incredible world of AI that's already here.

Welcome to your guide on stepping into this fascinating realm. The purpose of this book is simple: to equip you with the practical knowledge and tools to leverage generative AI, ChatGPT, and machine learning. Whether you're boosting your productivity, sparking creativity, or optimizing daily life, you'll find the essentials here.

In these pages, you'll discover practical applications that make a real difference. We'll explore top generative AI applications like ChatGPT,

Claude, Gemini, and more, diving into their capabilities and how they differ. We'll also touch on the fundamentals of prompt engineering, giving you templates and techniques to refine your skills. While theory will play a small role, the focus is on hands-on learning. You'll find detailed instructions and step-by-step exercises, making AI approachable and fun.

My vision for this book is to make AI accessible to everyone, especially beginners. I know firsthand how daunting AI can seem. But it doesn't have to be. My passion lies in breaking down complex concepts into bite-sized, digestible pieces. I want you to feel empowered, not overwhelmed.

So, who is this book for? It's for you, the curious beginner. You may have heard about AI but don't know where to start. Perhaps you want to enhance your personal or professional life with new skills. You're not alone. Many beginners feel intimidated by technical jargon or fear they need to know how to code. Rest assured, this book addresses these concerns head-on. You'll find clear explanations without the tech-speak.

AI has transformative potential in everyday life. Imagine automating mundane tasks, freeing up time for what truly matters. Picture using AI to brainstorm ideas or streamline your workflow. Understanding these technologies isn't just a skill—it's an opportunity. It opens doors to innovation and creativity.

Here are some key takeaways you can expect: you'll learn how to craft high-quality prompts, build your own AI assistant, and even explore monetization strategies. By the end of this book, you'll have a toolkit of skills ready to apply in various contexts.

I'm excited to invite you on this journey. Engage with the content, try the exercises, and apply the knowledge to your life. The more you put into it, the more you'll get out. This isn't just a book—it's a chance to transform how you interact with technology.

As you embark on this adventure, know I'm here to support you. I'm thrilled to guide you through the process and can't wait to see how you'll use AI to enhance your world. Let's dive in and see where this journey takes us.

1

UNDERSTANDING THE FUNDAMENTALS OF AI

Think about the first time you used a smartphone. Remember that moment when you swiped right, and the screen responded as if it knew exactly what you wanted? That's a tiny glimpse into the world of artificial intelligence, or AI, at work. AI might sound like something out of a sci-fi movie, but it's become an integral part of our daily lives. From helping you find the fastest route home on a GPS app to recommending the next binge-worthy series on Netflix, AI is the quiet force making our lives a little more seamless. Let's take a deeper look at what AI really is and how it does all these amazing things.

WHAT IS AI? DEMYSTIFYING THE BASICS

Artificial Intelligence, in its simplest form, is about machines performing tasks that, when done by humans, require intelligence. Imagine your computer being able to understand language, recognize patterns, or even learn from experience. That's AI. It's not magic; it's a combination of algorithms, data, and computing power working together. These machines, especially computers, are designed to mimic human cognitive functions like learning and problem-solving. Take virtual assistants like Siri or Alexa, for example. They understand your voice commands, process the information, and respond in a human-like manner. Or consider recommendation algorithms that suggest what you might like to watch next based on your viewing history. These everyday applications of AI make our lives easier and more personalized.

The journey of AI began in the 1950s, a time when the concept of machines with human-like intelligence was born. Pioneers like John McCarthy and Marvin Minsky laid the groundwork for AI's development. Fast forward to today, AI has evolved significantly from its humble beginnings. It has gone from simple programs capable of playing chess to complex systems that can analyze vast amounts of data in real time. This evolution reflects the rapid advancements in technology and the growing importance of AI in various sectors.

Now, let's talk about the different types of AI. You might hear terms like narrow AI and general AI thrown around. Narrow AI, which we encounter daily, is designed to perform specific tasks efficiently. Think of it as a specialist in a particular field. For instance, the virtual assistant on your smartphone is a type of narrow AI, as is facial recognition software. They excel at their designated tasks but can't perform beyond their programming. On the other hand, general AI is what you often see in movies—think J.A.R.V.I.S., Tony Stark's virtual assistant in Iron Man—a machine with human-like cognitive abilities capable of performing any intellectual task that a human can do. While narrow AI is already a reality, general AI remains theoretical, with researchers still working towards achieving this level of intelligence.

It's crucial to understand what AI can and cannot do. AI can process information faster than humans, making it invaluable in domains like data analysis and gaming. It can identify patterns and make predictions with impressive accuracy. However, AI isn't without limitations. It cannot truly understand context or emotion like a human does. Current technological constraints also limit AI's capacity to generalize knowledge across different domains. So, while AI is a powerful tool, it is not a replacement for human intelligence. It's more like an augmentative partner, assisting us in tasks where precision and speed are paramount.

At the core of AI are a few key components: algorithms, data, and processing power. Algorithms are sets of rules or instructions that AI follows to solve problems. They are the backbone of AI functionality, enabling machines to learn from data and make decisions. Data, on the other hand, is the fuel that powers AI. The quality and quantity of data determine how effectively AI can perform its tasks. High-quality data leads to more accurate outcomes, while poor data can skew results. Lastly, processing power refers to the computational capacity required to run AI models. As AI systems become more complex, they demand more processing power to function efficiently.

AI VS. MACHINE LEARNING: DISTINGUISHING THE DIFFERENCES

Think of artificial intelligence as the broad canvas of technology that aims to mimic human-like intelligence. On this canvas, machine learning is a vibrant stroke, a subset that empowers computers to learn from data rather than being explicitly programmed for every task. While AI encompasses everything from rule-based systems to complex decision-making processes, machine learning focuses on teaching computers to recognize patterns and make predictions based on data. It's the part of AI that enables your email to filter out spam or your streaming service to suggest the next great series.

Machine learning is a fascinating realm where computers can learn from experience. Instead of coding each step, we provide them with data and let them find patterns. Imagine teaching a child to recognize dogs by showing them pictures rather than explaining every feature. That's what machine learning does—algorithms like decision trees or neural networks identify patterns and make informed guesses. This ability to learn and adapt makes machine learning a powerhouse in predictive analytics. For instance, businesses use it to forecast sales trends or predict customer behavior, allowing them to make smarter, data-driven decisions.

Within machine learning, there are two main approaches: supervised and unsupervised learning. Supervised learning is akin to following a recipe with step-by-step instructions. We provide labeled data, like a set of images with tags indicating whether they contain a cat or a dog. The algorithm learns to distinguish between the two, refining its ability to recognize them in new images. This method is widely used in image recognition and language translation. On the other hand, unsupervised learning is more like exploring a new city without a map. Here, the algorithm is given data without explicit labels and must discover patterns independently. It's used for clustering, such as grouping customers based on purchasing behavior, helping businesses tailor their marketing strategies.

Understanding these distinctions is crucial for grasping AI's potential and limitations. Knowing how machine learning operates within AI opens up a world of possibilities across various industries. In finance, for instance, machine learning models assess credit risks and detect fraudulent activities, saving companies billions. In healthcare, these algorithms help in diagnosing diseases by analyzing medical images and patient data, leading to more accurate and timely treatments. The versatility of machine learning applications continues to grow, making it an invaluable tool in our increasingly data-driven world.

To see how integral machine learning is to AI, consider it the engine that powers many AI applications you use daily. While AI sets the stage for machines to mimic human intelligence, machine learning provides the specific skills needed to perform tasks efficiently. It's a symbiotic relationship where machine learning brings AI to life, making it practical and applicable to real-world challenges. This distinction not only highlights the dynamic nature of AI but also illustrates the incredible potential that machine learning holds in shaping the future.

THE ROLE OF DATA IN AI: UNDERSTANDING DATA SETS AND THEIR IMPORTANCE

Imagine trying to bake a cake without any ingredients. It wouldn't turn out well, would it? In the world of AI, data is the key ingredient. It's what fuels AI systems, driving their performance and accuracy. Without it, AI would be like a car without gas. It's the starting point for everything an AI system does. Data comes from various sources—think of the photos you upload, the searches you make, or even the weather apps that tell you if you need an umbrella. All these bits of information are collected, processed, and used to train AI models. But it's not just about having data; it's about having the right data. The quality of this data significantly impacts how well AI performs. Poor-quality data can lead to errors, while high-quality data can make AI systems incredibly accurate and reliable.

Data sets are collections of data that AI models use to learn. They can contain anything from numbers and text to images and sounds. A famous example is ImageNet, an extensive visual database designed to help AI recognize images. Data sets are like the textbooks AI reads to learn about the world. But before AI can use these data sets, they need to be cleaned and organized—a process known as data preprocessing. This involves removing errors, filling in missing values, and converting data into a format that AI systems can understand. It's a crucial step that ensures the accuracy of AI outputs and helps prevent any misinterpretations.

With the rise of AI, data privacy and ethics have become hot topics. How data is collected, stored, and used can have significant ethical implications. Regulations like the General Data Protection Regulation (GDPR) are in place to protect personal data and ensure it's used responsibly. But even with these safeguards, ethical dilemmas still arise. For instance, how much data is too much? Is it ethical to use personal data without explicit consent? These are questions that researchers and developers grapple with as they navigate the complex landscape of data ethics. It's a delicate balance between leveraging data for innovation and respecting personal privacy.

Bias in data is another critical concern. If the data used to train an AI model is biased, the outputs will also be biased. This can lead to unfair or misleading results. For example, facial recognition systems trained on data sets lacking diversity may perform poorly on certain demographics, leading to inaccurate identifications. This has real-world consequences and highlights the importance of using diverse and representative data sets. Strategies to mitigate data bias include careful data selection, thorough testing, and continuous monitoring to ensure fairness and accuracy. By addressing these biases, developers can create AI systems that are more equitable and reliable.

NEURAL NETWORKS FOR BEGINNERS: A SIMPLE EXPLANATION

Imagine your brain, a complex network of neurons firing and connecting, constantly processing information. This intricate system inspired the creation of neural networks in artificial intelligence. At their core, neural networks are algorithms that mimic the human brain's structure to recognize patterns and solve problems. They consist of layers of nodes, also known as neurons, which process input data and produce an output. Picture an assembly line in a factory, where each worker adds a part to the final product. Similarly, in a neural network, each neuron processes data and passes it to the next layer, gradually refining the information. This is the basic structure of a neural network.

Shallow neural networks have fewer layers and are used for more straightforward tasks, like basic image recognition. But when tasks become complex, deep neural networks come into play. These deep networks have multiple layers, allowing them to handle intricate problems by breaking them down into smaller, manageable parts. Think of them as a series of interconnected roads leading to your destination. The more roads you have, the more routes you can take to get there, making the journey smoother and more efficient. Deep neural networks are the backbone of deep learning, enabling technologies like self-driving cars and advanced voice assistants.

Neural networks learn through a process called training. During training, they adjust their internal parameters to minimize errors and improve accuracy. This is where backpropagation comes in. Backpropagation is like a teacher correcting a student's mistakes and guiding them to the right answers. It calculates the error between the predicted output and the actual result and then adjusts the network's parameters to reduce this error. An activation function further aids this process by determining which neurons should fire, adding complexity to the network's ability to learn. It's akin to deciding which lights to turn on in a room to create the perfect ambiance.

Neural networks have become integral to many everyday technologies. In image recognition, they can identify faces in photos or objects in a video. When you upload a picture on social media, a neural network might tag your friends automatically. They're also behind speech recognition systems, like the ones that transcribe your voice messages. Autonomous vehicles rely heavily on neural networks to perceive their surroundings, make decisions, and navigate roads safely. These networks process vast amounts of sensory data in real time, allowing vehicles to react quickly to changes in their environment.

Deep learning, a subset of machine learning, leverages deep neural networks to perform complex tasks that were once thought impossible. Unlike traditional machine learning, which relies on manual feature extraction, deep learning automatically discovers patterns and features in data. This capability makes it particularly powerful in fields like natural language processing, where it helps machines understand and generate human language. For instance, when you use a virtual assistant to set a reminder or ask for the weather, deep learning algorithms analyze your speech to provide accurate responses. It's also transforming industries like healthcare, where deep learning aids in diagnosing diseases by analyzing medical images.

In essence, neural networks have become a cornerstone of modern AI, driving innovations across various domains. They continue to evolve, unlocking new possibilities and expanding the boundaries of what machines can achieve. As you dive deeper into the world of AI, understanding neural networks will provide you with a solid foundation to appreciate the technology shaping our future.

BREAKING DOWN AI JARGON: A GLOSSARY FOR BEGINNERS

Navigating the world of artificial intelligence can often feel like deciphering a new language. The jargon can be intimidating, but let's break it down together. At the heart of AI is the "algorithm." Think of algorithms as step-by-step recipes that computers follow to solve problems or perform tasks. They're the instructions that tell an AI model, another key term, how to function. A "model" is the output of the training process, representing the knowledge the AI has learned. Speaking of "training," this is where an AI system learns from data, akin to studying for an exam. Imagine feeding a machine hundreds of photos of cats and dogs; through training, it learns to distinguish between them. But beware of "overfitting," where a model learns the training data too well, capturing noise as if it were a part of the pattern. This is like memorizing the answers to practice questions without understanding the underlying concepts. On the flip side, "underfitting" occurs when a model is too simple to capture the underlying trend, like a student who skimps on study time and misses key details.

Let's simplify some of the more complex terms you might encounter. "Natural Language Processing" or NLP, is the branch of AI that deals with the interaction between computers and humans using natural language. It's what enables your smartphone to understand and respond to your voice commands. Then there's "reinforcement learning," a type of machine learning where an agent learns how to behave in an environment by performing actions and receiving feedback. Picture training a dog: you reward it for sitting on command and ignore it when it jumps unnecessarily. Similarly, the AI learns to maximize positive outcomes based on the feedback it receives.

To make things more straightforward, let's use some examples. "Predictive analytics" is a term you might come across, and it's essentially about using data, statistical algorithms, and machine learning techniques to predict future outcomes based on historical data. Imagine weather forecasting, where computers analyze past weather patterns to predict tomorrow's storm. Then, there are machine learning models in recommendation systems, like those used by online retailers. When you shop online, the system suggests products based on your browsing history and the habits of similar users. This is AI at work, processing data to make educated guesses about what you might like.

Understanding these terms is more than just academic; it's practical for everyday discussions, especially as AI becomes more embedded in our lives. Whether you're chatting about the latest tech with friends or considering how AI can enhance your business, having a grasp of these concepts will boost your confidence and comprehension. It's like knowing the lingo when you travel to a new country—it helps you connect and engage with your surroundings more effectively. As AI continues to evolve, these terms will pop up in everything from news articles to tech talks, making it essential to have a foundational understanding. So, as you delve deeper into the fascinating world of AI, keep this glossary handy. It's your map to navigating the ever-growing landscape of artificial intelligence, helping you decode the complexities and truly appreciate the innovations at your fingertips.

ETHICAL IMPLICATIONS OF AI: BALANCING PROMISE AND PITFALLS

The rise of AI brings with it a host of ethical concerns, chief among them the fear of job displacement due to automation. Imagine a world where machines handle tasks traditionally done by humans, from factory floors to cashier counters. The efficiency and cost savings are undeniable, yet they pose a significant threat to employment. As AI systems become more prevalent, the workforce must adapt, potentially leading to a significant shift in job types and skill requirements. This shift may require extensive retraining and education programs to ensure workers can transition into new roles created by advancing technology. It's crucial that society addresses these concerns proactively, balancing innovation with the needs of the human workforce.

Privacy concerns also loom large in AI discussions, particularly regarding data collection. With AI's insatiable demand for data, questions arise about how much personal information is gathered and how it's utilized. For instance, AI-driven apps track our locations, preferences, and even conversations to offer personalized services. While this customization can enhance user experience, it raises significant privacy issues. Regulations like the GDPR aim to protect our data, but the challenge lies in ensuring compliance and safeguarding against misuse. The responsibility falls on AI developers and companies to maintain transparency and prioritize user consent, ensuring that data is handled ethically and securely.

AI's societal impacts extend beyond employment and privacy. In healthcare, AI's potential to revolutionize decision-making is immense. From diagnosing diseases to recommending treatments, AI systems can process vast amounts of medical data with precision. However, the reliance on AI raises questions about accountability and the human touch in medical care. Patients may wonder who is responsible for decisions made by AI and whether these systems can truly replace the nuanced judgment of experienced healthcare professionals. It's essential to strike a balance, using AI to augment, rather than replace, human expertise in healthcare settings.

On the social front, AI is reshaping how we communicate and interact. Social media platforms use AI to curate content and suggest connections, influencing our social dynamics and even our mental health. While these algorithms can create echo chambers, reinforcing existing beliefs, they also have the potential to bridge gaps and connect diverse communities. As AI becomes more integrated into our social fabric, we must remain vigilant about its influence, ensuring that it fosters genuine connection and understanding rather than division and isolation.

The promise of AI is vast, offering improvements in quality of life across various domains. From streamlining daily tasks to enabling breakthroughs in science and technology, AI has the potential to enhance human capabilities. Yet, with great power comes the risk of misuse and unintended consequences. Consider the potential for AI to be used in surveillance or warfare, raising ethical and moral dilemmas about its deployment. The challenge lies in harnessing AI's capabilities while mitigating its risks and ensuring that its benefits are shared equitably and responsibly.

Responsible AI development is key to addressing these challenges. Establishing ethical guidelines and frameworks can help steer AI development in a direction that prioritizes human values and societal well-being. Various organizations have set up AI ethics boards to oversee and guide the ethical deployment of AI technologies. These boards work to ensure that AI systems are transparent, accountable, and fair, minimizing biases and preventing harm. Examining case studies of ethical AI implementations can teach us valuable lessons in balancing innovation with responsibility. These examples illustrate how AI can be developed and used in ways that align with our collective aspirations and ethical standards.

As we continue to explore the potential of AI, it's essential to consider not only the technological advancements but also the ethical implications that accompany them. By fostering a culture of responsibility and accountability in AI development, we can ensure that this powerful technology serves as a force for good, enhancing our lives while respecting our values. The journey of AI is just beginning, and with thoughtful consideration and proactive measures, we can navigate its challenges and embrace its possibilities.

2
THE WORLD OF GENERATIVE AI

Imagine waking up to a world where your digital assistant not only knows your schedule but also anticipates your needs, setting the perfect morning playlist as you sip your coffee. This isn't a distant future; it's the power of generative AI transforming how we interact with technology.

OPENAI'S CHATGPT: THE GOLD STANDARD FOR GENERATIVE AI

At the heart of this transformation is a tool that's revolutionizing conversations: ChatGPT. Picture your favorite customer service interaction, where instead of waiting on hold, you're greeted by an AI that understands your query almost before you finish typing it. ChatGPT, developed by OpenAI, simulates human-like interactions, making mundane tasks feel personal and engaging.

ChatGPT excels in real-time customer support, allowing businesses to automate responses and streamline their service. Imagine logging onto a website and instantly engaging with a chatbot that not only understands your questions but also provides solutions seamlessly.

It draws on a vast knowledge base crafted from extensive training data to generate responses that feel natural and informative. Beyond customer service, ChatGPT has found its way into language translation, breaking down barriers and making communication across cultures smoother and more accessible. You can now chat with friends overseas, effortlessly translating your thoughts into their language, enhancing global connectivity.

The applications of ChatGPT stretch far and wide, touching various aspects of our lives. Businesses use it to enhance website user engagement, creating a more interactive and personalized browsing experience. Imagine landing on a site, and instead of sifting through endless FAQs, you interact with a friendly AI that guides you to the exact information you need. ChatGPT acts as a personal virtual assistant for individuals, managing your schedule, setting reminders, and even assisting in task management. It's like having a digital secretary who never sleeps, always ready to help you stay organized and productive.

One of the remarkable features of ChatGPT is its customization capabilities. Businesses can tailor the AI's response tone and style to align with their brand identity, ensuring consistency across customer interactions. Whether your brand is formal and professional or laid-back and friendly, ChatGPT can adapt its language to match, providing a cohesive experience for users. This flexibility makes it an invaluable tool for companies seeking to maintain a strong brand presence while automating customer interactions.

However, like any powerful tool, ChatGPT comes with its own set of challenges. One of the main concerns is the risk of misinformation. While ChatGPT can generate human-like responses, these responses require careful editing and fact-checking to ensure accuracy. The AI operates based on its training data, which means it might not always reflect the latest information or company policies. This necessitates a level of oversight to prevent the spread of incorrect information, especially in sensitive contexts.

Privacy is another critical issue, as ChatGPT interacts with users and potentially handles personal data. Ensuring that these interactions respect user privacy is paramount. Companies employing ChatGPT must implement robust data protection measures to safeguard personal information and comply with privacy regulations. Striking a balance between AI innovation and ethical considerations is essential to build trust with users and maintain the integrity of AI applications.

Reflection: Your Interaction with AI

Think about your last interaction with an AI. Was it an assistant on your phone, a chatbot on a website, or perhaps a language translation tool? Reflect on how it made the task easier or more engaging. Consider the possibilities of customizing such an AI to better fit your needs and how it might transform daily tasks. How do you feel about the privacy of your data during these interactions?

EXPLORING GOOGLE GEMINI: AI FOR PRODUCTIVITY

Imagine if creativity had a digital companion that could help shape your ideas and bring them to life. Enter Google Gemini, an AI tool that excels at generating creative writing content. This isn't just about automating mundane tasks but exploring new creative horizons. With Gemini, imagine crafting a poem that captures the essence of a sunset or developing a story that takes readers on an unexpected journey. It doesn't stop there. Gemini can assist in writing scripts and dialogues, providing suggestions that might spark your next big idea. This AI tool is like a brainstorming partner, always ready to offer fresh perspectives and innovative twists.

The creative process can be daunting, especially when writer's block strikes. We've all faced that blank page, unsure of where to start. This is where Gemini comes in. It generates prompts that kickstart your imagination, offering themes or ideas that might not have crossed your mind. Think of it as a gentle nudge to get your creative juices flowing. But it's not just about starting; Gemini can also keep the momentum going. During brainstorming sessions, it collaborates with you, suggesting plot twists or character developments, turning the solitary act of writing into a dynamic partnership. It's like having a co-writer who never tires and is always ready to contribute.

One of Gemini's standout features is its ability to adapt its writing style to suit different genres and audiences. Are you crafting a young adult fiction novel? Gemini can tailor its tone to resonate with younger readers, using language and themes that capture their attention. Or you're mixing genres, creating a narrative that blends fantasy with a touch of mystery. Gemini can seamlessly shift its style, helping you create unique narrative experiences that defy traditional storytelling boundaries. This adaptability ensures that the AI tool complements your vision rather than overshadowing it, allowing your unique voice to shine through.

Beyond text, Gemini is a multimodal AI, supporting interactions through voice and images, making it incredibly versatile. This means it can be used for tasks requiring different data inputs and outputs, such as multimedia content creation. Imagine working on a digital project where you need to integrate text, audio, and visuals. Gemini can assist in crafting cohesive content that engages audiences across multiple platforms. It's like having a Swiss Army knife of creativity, ready to tackle any challenge you throw its way.

Gemini doesn't operate in isolation; it seamlessly integrates with Google Services like Google Docs, Gmail, and other applications within the Google ecosystem. This integration enhances productivity, streamlining tasks like email management and document editing. Imagine drafting an email where Gemini suggests ways to make your message more compelling or working on a document where it highlights areas for improvement. This union between AI and existing tools makes for a smoother workflow, allowing you to focus on what truly matters—creating content that resonates with your audience.

CLAUDE BY ANTHROPIC: EMPOWERING AI FOR DATA ANALYSIS

Claude by Anthropic stands out like a beacon for those who deal with extensive data in the ever-expanding landscape of artificial intelligence. Imagine an AI that can seamlessly handle up to 1,000,000 tokens of information. This capacity makes Claude ideal for processing large-scale data inputs and engaging in comprehensive interactions. Whether you're working on complex datasets for scientific research or need in-depth analysis for business decisions, Claude offers an unparalleled ability to manage and interpret vast amounts of information efficiently. It's like having a super-powered assistant who never tires, ready to tackle the most intricate data challenges.

What sets Claude apart are its specialized models, each designed for specific tasks. Think of them as a team of experts, each with a distinct focus. There's Haiku for quick tasks, Sonnet for moderate complexity, and Opus for in-depth analysis. This diversity of models allows Claude to cater to a wide range of needs, from simple data extraction to complex reasoning and coding tasks. It's like having a toolbox where you can pick the exact tool needed for the job, ensuring precision and efficiency in every task you undertake.

For developers and those engaged in programming, Claude shines brightly. Its prowess in coding tasks and optical character recognition (OCR) is exceptional. Imagine working on a project that involves extracting data from images or needing to code a complex program. Claude not only provides accurate outputs but does so reliably, reducing the margin for error significantly. This capability makes it an indispensable asset for anyone involved in detailed programming or data extraction from visual sources. It's like having a second pair of eyes that never miss a detail, enhancing accuracy and productivity.

Beyond its technical capabilities, Claude is noted for its ethical AI practices. In a world where ethical considerations are paramount, Claude's adherence to guidelines ensures that interactions remain safe and free from bias. Its low refusal rates mean fewer instances where the AI fails to process requests, ensuring smooth and reliable operations. This focus on ethical standards is crucial, especially when dealing with sensitive data or making decisions that impact users' lives. It's like having a trusted advisor who not only performs their tasks well but does so with integrity and responsibility.

Case Study: Claude in Action

Consider a marketing firm needing to analyze customer interaction data to improve conversion rates. Using Claude, they can quickly process extensive datasets, gaining insights that inform strategic decisions. Claude's ability to handle large data volumes allows the team to identify patterns and trends that might be invisible with manual analysis, leading to improved customer engagement strategies and increased sales. This example illustrates Claude's potential in real-world applications, transforming how businesses approach data analysis and decision-making.

Claude by Anthropic is more than just another AI tool; it's a powerful ally in the realm of data analysis. Its ability to handle complex tasks with ease, combined with its ethical approach, makes it a standout choice for anyone looking to leverage AI in handling extensive data.

COPILOT: ENHANCING PRODUCTIVITY WITH AI ASSISTANCE

Microsoft Copilot integrates seamlessly into the Microsoft 365 suite, enhancing productivity across various applications. It's embedded in

Word, Excel, PowerPoint, Outlook, Teams, and other Microsoft 365 apps, offering AI-powered assistance for a wide range of tasks.

In Word, Copilot helps draft documents, generate ideas, and summarize content. Excel users benefit from data analysis, formula generation, and insight identification. PowerPoint integration allows for quick presentation creation and organization. Outlook users can manage emails more efficiently, while Teams benefits from improved collaboration and communication tools.

Have you ever been knee-deep in a coding project and wished for an extra pair of hands? Enter Copilot, designed to boost productivity by automating those repetitive coding tasks that often slow development. Imagine having an intelligent assistant that can predict your next line of code, suggest improvements, or even complete entire functions based on your coding style. It's like having a seasoned developer whispering the best practices in your ear, cutting down the time spent on mundane tasks, and letting you focus on the creative aspects of software development. Copilot doesn't just speed up coding; it enhances overall efficiency, helping you meet deadlines with greater ease and precision.

But Copilot's magic extends beyond individual productivity. It also plays a significant role in facilitating teamwork and collaboration within development teams. Consider the complexities of project management, where coordination and communication are key. AI-assisted tools integrated with Copilot can streamline these processes, providing project managers with insights that help allocate resources and manage timelines effectively. In a team setting, Copilot assists in collaborative code review and debugging, allowing team members to work on the same codebase without stepping on each other's toes. It highlights areas that need attention, suggests improvements, and ensures that the code is functional but also robust and efficient.

In real-world settings, Copilot's applications are vast and varied. For instance, a tech company can streamline document creation and editing by suggesting templates or generating reports based on data analysis. Imagine a scenario where a business analyst must compile a comprehensive client report. Copilot can sift through data, identify trends, and produce a coherent document in a fraction of the time it would take manually. This capability extends to data analysis and reporting, where AI-driven insights can reveal patterns and inform strategic decisions. It's like having a personal assistant with the analytical prowess of a seasoned researcher, providing you with actionable insights at your fingertips.

However, it's essential to consider the potential drawbacks that come with relying heavily on AI for productivity. One concern is the risk of skill atrophy. Suppose developers become too dependent on AI for coding. In that case, they might lose the edge on their problem-solving skills and coding proficiency. Maintaining a balance is crucial, as is using AI to enhance skills rather than replace them.

Additionally, security concerns in AI-assisted environments cannot be ignored. As Copilot integrates deeply with development workflows, ensuring that the AI systems are secure and compliant with industry standards is essential. This involves safeguarding sensitive data and maintaining strict access controls to prevent unauthorized use.

As you explore the possibilities with Copilot, remember that it's a tool designed to augment your capabilities, not replace them. Embrace its potential to automate repetitive tasks and enhance productivity, but keep honing your skills and staying attuned to the ever-evolving landscape of technology. The key is finding harmony between human ingenuity and AI efficiency, ensuring that each complements the other to achieve remarkable results.

UNVEILING PERPLEXITY AI: A NEW FRONTIER IN INFORMATION DISCOVERY

Perplexity AI emerges as a powerful tool that revolutionizes how we interact with information, offering a range of capabilities that cater to diverse needs. As an advanced answer engine, it surpasses traditional search engines by providing direct, comprehensive responses to complex queries, complete with cited sources. This feature eliminates the need to sift through multiple search results, saving time and ensuring accuracy.

Example Prompt: "What are the health benefits of a low-carb diet?"

Perplexity will generate a response with references from medical journals, expert articles, and research studies.

One of Perplexity's standout features is its ability to track real-time events, offering up-to-the-minute updates on everything from stock market trends to election results. This capability keeps users informed about breaking news and live events, making it an invaluable resource for those who need to stay ahead of the curve.

Example Prompt: "What's the latest on Nvidia's stock performance today?"

Perplexity will provide up-to-the-minute data with sources from financial news outlets.

For savvy shoppers, Perplexity serves as an efficient price comparison tool. By aggregating data from various e-commerce platforms, it quickly identifies the best deals, streamlining the shopping process and potentially saving users money.

Example Prompt: "Where can I find the best price for the latest Samsung Galaxy?"

Perplexity will fetch prices from Amazon, Best Buy, and other retailers.

Content creators and researchers benefit from Perplexity's summarization capabilities. The AI can distill lengthy articles or research papers into concise summaries, extracting key points without losing essential details. This feature is handy for professionals needing to process large amounts of information quickly.

Paste a link or input text and include a prompt, and Perplexity will generate a concise summary.

Example Prompt: "Summarize this ChatGPT article on academic writing."

Perplexity will condense the insights into an easy-to-read format.

Perplexity is a valuable asset for traders and investors in the financial sector. It provides real-time stock prices, financial reports, and market trends, enabling users to make informed decisions based on the latest data.

Example Prompt: "What's the latest financial report for Meta?"

Perplexity will provide revenue updates, profit margins, and market insights.

For digital marketers and content creators, Perplexity offers SEO optimization tools. It can generate keyword ideas, topic clusters, and content suggestions to improve search engine rankings. This functionality is crucial for businesses and individuals looking to enhance online visibility.

Example Prompt: "Generate a list of keywords for a title for a book about optimizing work productivity."

Perplexity will provide keyword clusters with search intent analysis.

Perplexity also aids in creative writing and content generation, helping users overcome writer's block by providing ideas, outlines, and even draft content for various purposes. This feature is handy for bloggers, marketers, and content creators who must consistently produce engaging material.

Example Prompt: "Give me 10 blog post ideas about meal prepping."

Perplexity will generate engaging and SEO-friendly topic suggestions.

The AI's versatility extends to its multimodal capabilities, allowing users to interact through text, voice, and images. This feature enhances its utility across various applications, from content creation to complex problem-solving.

Perplexity's context awareness sets it apart, enabling it to understand and build upon previous queries for more natural, conversational interactions. This capability allows for a more intuitive and efficient user experience.

While Perplexity offers numerous advantages, it's important to note that it may have limitations in certain areas, such as the immediacy of updates for live events compared to some specialized platforms. However, its continuous development and improvement suggest that these limitations may be addressed in future updates.

Perplexity AI represents a significant advancement in AI-powered information retrieval and processing. Its diverse capabilities make it a valuable tool for many users, from students and researchers to professionals and content creators. It offers a glimpse into the future of AI-assisted information management and content creation.

XAI'S GROK AND DEEPSEEK: REVOLUTIONIZING AI WITH REBELLIOUS INTELLIGENCE AND ENTERPRISE PRECISION

Grok differs from other generative AI platforms in its real-time knowledge acquisition capabilities, leveraging data from the X platform to provide up-to-date responses. Unlike ChatGPT, which uses

GPT-4 models trained on data up to September 2022, Grok has access to more recent information. Grok-1 outperforms models like GPT-3.5 and Meta's LLaMa 2 in certain benchmarks, though it still falls short of GPT-4 in overall performance.

Grok is designed with a unique personality, incorporating humor and wit into its responses. It excels in technical jargon and specific tasks, while ChatGPT is noted for its conversational skills and coherence. Grok also offers image generation capabilities using the FLUX.1 model, a feature not present in ChatGPT. In short, Grok 3 leans into immediacy and attitude, while ChatGPT-4 leads in sophistication, versatility, and broader real-world application.

DeepSeek represents a groundbreaking approach to artificial intelligence development, distinguished by its innovative strategies and unique technological capabilities. Emerging from the Chinese AI ecosystem, the platform has distinguished itself through a remarkably cost-effective development model, achieving high-performance results with substantially lower investment compared to U.S. competitors.

The model's architectural design leverages a sophisticated 'mixture-of-experts' approach, dynamically activating only the most relevant computational submodels for specific tasks. This strategy enables unprecedented computational efficiency and nuanced problem-solving capabilities. Unlike many proprietary AI platforms, DeepSeek has committed to an open-source philosophy, sharing its algorithmic frameworks and training methodologies transparently.

DeepSeek's models demonstrate exceptional prowess in complex reasoning tasks, particularly in mathematical computations and programming challenges. By implementing advanced "chain-of-thought" reasoning techniques, the AI can deconstruct intricate problems with remarkable precision. The platform's emphasis on explainable AI ensures users can understand the underlying logic behind its responses, a critical feature distinguishing it from more opaque generative models.

DeepSeek's holistic approach to AI development truly sets it apart—prioritizing software-driven efficiency, adaptability, and collaborative innovation. By focusing on maximizing algorithmic potential rather than relying exclusively on advanced hardware, DeepSeek has rapidly emerged as a formidable competitor in the global AI landscape.

MIDJOURNEY: CREATING VISUAL MASTERPIECES WITH AI

Imagine having the power to create stunning visual content with just a few clicks. Midjourney is an AI tool that makes this a reality, focusing on generating high-quality visuals that captivate and inspire. Midjourney, operating through Discord, is widely regarded as one of the best AI text prompt-to-image generation tools available. Whether you're into designing intricate landscapes or conceptualizing futuristic architecture, Midjourney offers a canvas for creativity that blends technology with artistry. Picture yourself crafting fashion patterns that could grace the runways of Paris or textile designs that redefine luxury and comfort. Midjourney is like having an artist's studio in your pocket, ready to turn your visions into tangible masterpieces.

The creative industries are buzzing with possibilities thanks to Midjourney's capabilities. In advertising, imagine launching a campaign with visuals so compelling they stop scrollers in their tracks. Midjourney can produce AI-generated visuals that resonate with audiences, making your message unforgettable. In film and animation, it's a game-changer during pre-production design, allowing creators to visualize scenes and characters with unparalleled detail and imagination. Visual storytelling reaches new heights as artists explore narrative possibilities previously confined to the imagination, now brought to life with vivid accuracy and flair.

One of Midjourney's most exciting features is its ability to produce diverse visual styles. Whether you're aiming for a minimalist aesthetic or something more ornate, Midjourney provides customizable settings to align with your artistic direction. This flexibility extends to its integration with 3D modeling software, enabling creators to add depth and dimension to their projects. Envision crafting a virtual world where every detail is meticulously designed, from the grandest structures to the smallest textures. Midjourney doesn't just create visuals; it elevates them, offering tools that let your creative spirit soar.

However, as with any innovation, AI-generated visuals bring their own set of ethical considerations. Ownership and copyright are at the forefront, raising questions about who owns AI-generated art. If an AI assists in creating a piece, does the credit go to the artist, the AI, or both? These questions challenge traditional views and call for new frameworks that respect human creativity and technological contribution. Moreover, the ethical use of AI in visual media production must be considered. Ensuring that AI serves as a tool for positive creation, rather than manipulation or deception, is crucial in maintaining the integrity of visual storytelling.

As we navigate the world of AI-generated visuals, we must strike a balance between innovation and ethics. Midjourney opens doors to creative possibilities that are as exciting as they are unprecedented. It invites artists to explore new frontiers while remaining mindful of the implications of their creations. The potential to redefine industries and reshape artistic boundaries is immense, yet it must be approached with a sense of responsibility and awareness. Midjourney is a testament to what can be achieved when creativity and technology converge in this dynamic landscape.

DALL-E AND FIREFLY: GENERATING IMAGERY WITH AI

DALL-E 3 represents a significant leap forward in AI image generation technology, offering users unprecedented capabilities in creating visual content. Developed by OpenAI, the platform has dramatically improved over its previous iterations, demonstrating an enhanced understanding of prompts and superior image generation quality. The AI's core strength lies in its ability to accurately interpret complex textual descriptions. Unlike earlier versions, DALL-E 3 can generate images that closely match user prompts, handling nuanced details in color, contrast, and composition. It is particularly adept at creating professional-quality visual content across various domains.

For businesses, DALL-E 3 provides a cost-effective solution for generating visual materials. Users can create unique logos, compelling product packaging, advertisement posters, and social media graphics without requiring extensive design skills. Journalists and content creators can also leverage the tool to produce engaging infographics and visual storytelling elements.

OpenAI has also prioritized safety and ethical considerations. The platform includes robust mechanisms to prevent generating harmful content, decline requests involving public figures, and mitigate potential biases. Additionally, creators can opt out of having their images used in future training datasets.

A standout feature is DALL-E 3's integration with ChatGPT, allowing users to refine prompts collaboratively. This interactive approach enables more precise image generation, with the AI helping to brainstorm and improve initial concepts. The platform is accessible through ChatGPT and available to developers via API, making it a versatile tool for individual creators and professional applications.

Adobe Firefly's core strength lies in its seamless integration within Adobe's Creative Cloud ecosystem, enabling creators to generate, modify, and enhance visual content across Photoshop, Illustrator,

Express, and Premiere Pro. Its text-to-image generation capabilities allow users to transform textual descriptions into sophisticated visual representations. At the same time, generative fill features provide unprecedented flexibility in image manipulation. What distinguishes Firefly is its commitment to commercial safety and ethical AI development. Unlike many generative AI platforms, Adobe has meticulously trained its models on licensed content, addressing critical copyright concerns that have plagued similar technologies. This approach ensures creators can confidently use AI-generated content in professional environments.

The latest Firefly Image 3 model, released in April 2024, demonstrates remarkable improvements in image quality, generation speed, and prompt comprehension. Users can now easily create complex visual narratives, from intricate vector graphics to photorealistic imagery and even experimental video content. Adobe's strategic positioning of Firefly reflects a broader vision of democratizing creative technologies. By offering free and premium plans with varying generative credits, the platform makes advanced AI tools accessible to individual creators and large enterprises. As AI continues to reshape creative industries, Adobe Firefly stands at the forefront, transforming how professionals conceptualize, design, and produce digital content.

Here are a few examples of the awesome power of AI text-to-image generation.

Prompt: A woman's lifelike portrait showcasing her vibrant personality, adorned in bohemian attire with intricate patterns. The setting is a sunlit meadow filled with wildflowers, enhancing the natural and organic feel. — ar 3:4 — style raw

Prompt: A busy Shibuya street at night, neon lights reflecting off wet pavement. Captured with a Sony A7R IV + 35mm f/1.4 lens, slow shutter (1/15s) to create motion blur of pedestrians.

Prompt: Photorealistic image of a white owl

MUSIC MAKERS: A DEEP DIVE INTO BOOMY AND SOUNDRAW

Picture yourself as a budding musician with a melody in your head but no idea how to bring it to life. Enter Boomy and Soundraw, two AI platforms transforming music creation into an accessible and enjoyable process for everyone. Boomy's user-friendly interface makes it a perfect starting point for novices. You don't need to read music or play an instrument. Select your desired mood or genre, and Boomy takes care of the rest, composing tracks that sound like seasoned artists have crafted them. It's as if you've got a personal music studio at your fingertips, ready to produce melodies that match your creative spirit.

Soundraw, on the other hand, caters to more experienced musicians, offering adaptability that meets professional needs. With Soundraw, you can tweak compositions to suit specific projects, adjusting tempo, instrumentation, and dynamics with precision. This customization allows musicians to create tracks that align perfectly with their artistic vision, whether a haunting piano solo or an energetic electronic beat. The platform's intuitive design ensures that even complex compositions can be easily crafted. It is a valuable tool for those who demand creativity and control in their music-making.

When it comes to the quality and variety of music these platforms generate, the range is impressive. Boomy and Soundraw cover genres from classical to hip-hop, offering an extensive palette for users to explore. Each track can be customized to reflect your unique style, whether you're crafting an upbeat pop anthem or a soothing ambient piece. This versatility means that musicians can experiment with different sounds, pushing the boundaries of traditional music genres and discovering new sonic landscapes that resonate with their audience.

These AI tools are democratizing music production, making it possible for anyone with a computer to create their own tracks. It's a DIY revolution, empowering amateurs to produce music without the high costs or technical barriers traditionally associated with the industry. Whether you're a hobbyist looking to create a personal soundtrack or an aspiring artist recording your first album, Boomy and Soundraw open doors that were once exclusive to those with access to professional studios and equipment.

However, the rise of AI in music production also brings challenges and considerations. Traditional music producers and composers may feel the impact as AI-generated music becomes more prevalent. The question of originality arises—can a melody composed by AI be considered truly original, or does it borrow too heavily from existing works? Ethical concerns over royalties and ownership must be addressed, ensuring that artists are fairly compensated for their contributions, even when AI plays a role in the creative process.

AI-generated music offers opportunities and challenges in this evolving landscape, reshaping how we think about creation and collaboration. As you explore the potential of Boomy and Soundraw, consider how these tools might enhance your musical journey, whether you're composing for fun or aiming to break into the industry. The fusion of technology and creativity in music is just one example of how AI is reshaping artistic expression, leading us into a future where anyone can be a creator.

As we close this chapter, remember that the world of generative AI is vast and full of potential. With each tool we've explored, from ChatGPT to Boomy, a new dimension of creativity unfolds. In the next chapter, we'll delve into the practical applications of these technologies in everyday life, from enhancing productivity to sparking innovation.

3
PROMPT ENGINEERING ESSENTIALS

Picture this: you're trying to communicate with a friend who speaks a different language, and all you have is a translation app. The words you choose must be clear and precise for your message to make sense. This scenario mirrors the art of prompt engineering, a skill at the heart of interacting effectively with AI. Prompt engineering is about crafting the correct queries to guide AI systems like ChatGPT or Claude, ensuring they understand your intent and provide helpful responses. It's the bridge that connects your ideas with the AI's capabilities, transforming vague thoughts into clear instructions.

When crafting prompts, clarity and specificity cannot be overstated. Imagine asking a chef to make you a dish without specifying what you want. The result could be anything. Similarly, a vague prompt might confuse the AI, leading to irrelevant or incomplete answers. To get the best results, your prompts should be like a well-written recipe—detailed and specific. This clarity helps the AI understand the task at hand, reducing the chances of misinterpretation and enhancing the reliability of its responses. Context plays a crucial role, too. Just like a story needs a setting, your prompts need context to guide AI in the right direction. Without it, even the most advanced AI can stray off course.

The value of well-crafted prompts lies in their ability to improve AI efficiency. Imagine asking your AI assistant to "find information." Without specifics, it might provide a broad and unfocused response. On the other hand, a prompt like "summarize the latest news in renewable energy" directs the AI to a specific task, yielding a more relevant and valuable output. This precision saves time and enhances the relevance of the AI's response. Poorly crafted prompts lead to frustration and inefficiency, while thoughtfully designed ones streamline interactions and maximize the AI's potential.

Several key principles guide effective prompt engineering. Clarity is paramount—use concise and direct language to avoid ambiguity. Relevance ensures that every word in your prompt serves a purpose, aligning with your desired outcome. Engagement involves crafting prompts that convey your intent and resonate with the AI's strengths, encouraging it to perform at its best. Focusing on these principles creates a foundation for successful AI interactions. It's about speaking the AI's language and ensuring your instructions are as clear and engaging as possible.

Prompt engineering has come a long way since the early days of AI. Initially, interactions were limited to simple commands, akin to giving directions to a basic GPS. As AI technology has advanced, so too have the prompts we use. Today, they are more sophisticated and capable of guiding AI through complex tasks and nuanced conversations. This evolution reflects the growing capabilities of AI systems, which now handle a wider range of applications. Looking forward, the future of prompt engineering is bright, with trends pointing towards even more intuitive and dynamic interactions. As AI continues to evolve, the art of crafting prompts will become increasingly important, shaping how we harness this technology in our personal and professional lives.

Here are a few prompts to help you think about how including specificity and clarity in your prompts can guide your GPT to produce a helpful response.

1. Requesting an Explanation

Poor Prompt:

"Tell me about AI."

Well-Crafted Prompt:

"Can you provide a concise explanation of artificial intelligence (AI), including its main types (narrow AI and general AI) and a few real-world applications?"

2. Seeking a Recipe

Poor Prompt:

"Give me a recipe."

Well-Crafted Prompt:

"Can you provide a simple, high-protein chicken recipe with minimal ingredients that takes less than 30 minutes to prepare?"

3. Asking for Writing Help

Poor Prompt:

"Help me write something about leadership."

Well-Crafted Prompt:

"Can you help me write a 200-word persuasive paragraph on why emotional intelligence is crucial for effective leadership in corporate environments?"

4. Generating a Workout Plan

Poor Prompt:

"Give me a workout."

Well-Crafted Prompt:

"Can you design a 4-week strength training program focused on muscle gain for someone who is 5'8 ", 150 lbs, and moderately active, aiming to gain 10 lbs of muscle?"

5. Asking for a Business Idea

Poor Prompt:

"What's a good business idea?"

Well-Crafted Prompt:

"Can you suggest a profitable online business idea that requires minimal startup costs and can be managed remotely, along with key steps to get started?"

The poorly written prompts in these examples are too vague and generalized, and they will most likely produce irrelevant or unhelpful responses.

Each well-crafted prompt provides specificity, context, clarity, and a defined expectation for the response.

BASIC PROMPT TECHNIQUES: FOUNDATIONS FOR SUCCESS

Let's talk about the nuts and bolts of crafting effective AI prompts. Imagine you're preparing a shopping list for someone else to buy groceries. You wouldn't just write "food," right? Similarly, when crafting prompts, aim for precision and clarity. One foundational technique is using instructional language. Think of it as giving directions to a friend who's never been to your house. You'd use clear, step-by-step guidance to lead them to your front door. Your prompts should do the same for AI, clearly outlining your needs. This method helps avoid confusion and ensures your AI tool understands your intent.

Incorporating specific keywords is another powerful technique. When you tell someone exactly what you want, like "ripe avocados" instead of just "avocados," you're more likely to get what you need. The same goes for prompts. Specificity reduces ambiguity, guiding the AI to focus on the most relevant aspects of your request. This precision doesn't just help the AI; it also helps you by improving the quality of the response. You'll find that the more specific your language, the more accurate and valuable the AI's output becomes. It's like setting a GPS with an exact address instead of a vague area.

Let's explore some common pitfalls in prompt creation. Ambiguity is a frequent offender. Imagine asking, "Can you help?" without any context. The AI might not know where to start. Such leading prompts can leave too much to interpretation, resulting in broad or irrelevant responses. Another mistake is overloading prompts with unnecessary details or multiple tasks, confusing the AI. Keeping your prompts direct and focused helps avoid these pitfalls. Remember, the goal is to communicate as clearly with AI as you would with someone who knows nothing about the task.

To practice these techniques, try crafting prompts for everyday tasks. Start simple, like asking an AI assistant to "set a reminder for my doctor's appointment at 3 PM on Friday." Then, refine it: "Set a reminder for my doctor's appointment on Friday at 3 PM, and notify me an hour before." Notice how the refined prompt adds clarity and ensures you get the alert when you need it. Or, practice with a scheduling task, such as "Find a time for a meeting with Tom and Sue next week." Refine it to include specific days and times, making it easier for the AI to suggest options.

In the real world, these basic techniques have a variety of applications. Consider customer service chatbots. They rely on well-crafted prompts to guide interactions and provide accurate information. A prompt like "Tell me about your return policy" is straightforward and likely to yield a precise answer. Similarly, in educational AI applications, prompts help tailor learning experiences. A student might type, "Explain photosynthesis simply," prompting the AI to offer a breakdown that's easy to understand. These examples illustrate how foundational techniques enhance user experience across diverse contexts.

Prompt crafting may seem simple, but it's a skill that requires practice and attention to detail. The ability to communicate effectively with AI can transform how you use technology, making interactions smoother and more productive. As you become more comfortable with these techniques, you'll find that your prompts become more natural and intuitive, allowing you to get the most out of your AI tools without any hassle.

ADVANCED PROMPT TECHNIQUES: BEYOND THE BASICS

As you gain confidence in crafting prompts, diving into more advanced techniques can significantly enhance your interactions with AI. Consider the concept of layering prompts for multi-step responses. Just like building a tower, each layer or prompt adds depth, guiding the AI to handle complex tasks effectively. For instance, if you're working on a project requiring multiple stages of analysis, layering prompts can help the AI process each step in order, ensuring nothing gets overlooked. This approach transforms a single, overwhelming task into manageable segments, making it easier for both you and the AI to achieve the desired result.

Example of a Layered Prompt (Project Management Plan in One Step)

"Can you outline a project plan for developing a mobile app, including key milestones, budget allocation, team resources, and performance metrics for tracking success?"

Why It's Layering? Multiple aspects (milestones, budget, resources, metrics) are requested in a single prompt rather than broken into steps.

Another powerful tool in your prompt crafting kit is implementing conditional logic. Think of it as setting rules or conditions the AI must follow, like programming a simple "if-then" statement. This technique allows you to tailor responses based on specific criteria, ensuring the AI adapts to changing requirements. For example, if you're managing customer inquiries, you might use conditional logic to guide the AI in providing different responses based on the customer's location or product interest. This adaptability enhances the AI's ability to provide relevant, context-aware outcomes, making interactions more precise and efficient.

Customization plays a vital role in maximizing the effectiveness of your prompts. Tailoring prompts for different AI models is akin to adjusting your approach based on the tools at your disposal. Just as you would use different brushes for painting on various surfaces, customizing prompts ensure they align with the strengths and limitations of each AI model. This involves understanding the unique capabilities of the AI you're working with and adapting your prompts to leverage those strengths.

Example of a Tailored Prompt

General Prompt (Not Tailored):

"Give me a workout plan."

Tailored Prompt:

*"Can you design a **4-week strength training program** for a **moderately active individual** who is **5'8 ", 150 lbs, and aiming to gain 10 lbs of muscle**? The plan should include **progressive overload, compound exercises, and a focus on protein intake** to support muscle growth."*

Why This Works:

Specific Goal → Muscle gain, 10 lbs in 4 weeks

User Profile → Weight, height, and activity level included

Training Focus → Strength training with progressive overload

Additional Considerations → Nutrition guidance (protein intake)

A tailored prompt removes ambiguity and ensures the response is precise, relevant, and actionable.

To hone these advanced techniques, consider engaging in exercises that challenge your problem-solving skills. Design prompts for complex scenarios, such as simulating a multi-stage business negotiation or crafting a series of prompts to guide an AI through a detailed research analysis. These exercises encourage creative thinking and help you explore the full potential of prompt engineering. Iterative testing of these prompts will refine your skills as you learn to adjust and optimize based on the AI's performance and outcomes.

In specialized fields, advanced prompt techniques open up exciting possibilities. In AI-driven research and analysis, for example, tailored prompts can guide AI systems through intricate data sets, extracting meaningful insights and identifying trends. This capability transforms raw data into actionable intelligence, empowering researchers to make informed decisions. Similarly, in creative content generation, advanced prompts can inspire AI to contribute innovative ideas or assist in developing complex narratives. Whether you're brainstorming a new marketing campaign or crafting a novel, these techniques expand the boundaries of what's possible with AI-generated content.

As you explore these advanced techniques, remember that practice and experimentation are key. Don't hesitate to push the limits and try new approaches, even if they seem unconventional. The flexibility and adaptability of AI models make them ideal partners in your creative and analytical endeavors, offering support as you tackle increasingly complex challenges. By embracing these techniques, you unlock new levels of potential in your AI interactions, transforming how you approach tasks and maximize outcomes.

20 ESSENTIAL TEMPLATES FOR AI PROMPTS

Let's talk about templates. Think of them as the recipe cards for cooking up effective AI interactions. They provide a structured way to create prompts that make sense and are efficient and effective. Having diverse templates at your fingertips can transform how you interact with AI, whether you're extracting data or brainstorming new ideas. For instance, a template designed for data extraction might include fields for specifying the data type, source, and desired format, ensuring the AI understands precisely what you need. On the flip side, templates for creative brainstorming might include prompts to generate ideas for a marketing campaign or plot twists for a novel. These templates act as starting points, guiding you through the prompt creation process with ease.

Customization is the key to making these templates truly work for you. Just like you might tweak a recipe to suit your taste, you can modify templates to fit specific contexts and needs. You might be in marketing, education, or any other field—each has unique requirements. Maybe you're working on a project that requires industry-specific jargon or a particular tone. Adjusting the template to include these elements can make your AI prompts more targeted and relevant. Incorporating user input is another way to refine a template. By gathering feedback from those who interact with the AI, you can modify prompts to better align with their expectations and improve overall satisfaction. It's about making the template fit like a glove, ensuring that the AI outputs are as close to perfect as possible.

To see these templates in action, consider how they might be used in various scenarios. In marketing, a template could help craft prompts for an AI to generate social media posts, complete with hashtags and calls to action. This approach streamlines content creation, saving time and ensuring consistency across platforms. In educational settings, templates can guide AI in developing personalized learning plans or creating quizzes tailored to individual student needs. Imagine a teacher using a template to prompt an AI to design a lesson plan incorporating multimedia resources and interactive activities, enhancing student engagement and learning outcomes. These examples illustrate the versatility of templates and their potential to revolutionize different aspects of work and learning.

Experimentation is where the magic happens. Testing variations of templates can reveal new ways to optimize results and achieve even greater precision in AI responses. Think of it as a playground for creativity, where you can try different combinations to see what works best. Maybe altering the sequence of questions in a template leads to more insightful data analysis, or adding a specific keyword enhances the depth of a brainstorming session. The possibilities are endless, and the only limit is your imagination. By encouraging experimentation, you improve the templates and deepen your understanding of how AI thinks and operates. This process transforms prompt engineering from a static task into a dynamic exploration of possibilities.

Here are **20 well-crafted prompt templates** that can easily be customized by filling in their specific details. Each template ensures clarity, specificity, and structure for better responses.

1. Explain a Concept

"Can you explain ***[concept/topic]*** *in simple terms for someone with* ***[beginner/intermediate/advanced]*** *knowledge?"*

2. Compare Two Things

"What are the key differences and similarities between ***[thing 1]*** *and* ***[thing 2]****, and which one is better for* ***[specific use case]****?"*

3. Generate a Meal Plan

"Can you create a ***[number]-day*** *meal plan that is* ***[diet type: high-protein, vegan, keto, etc.]*** *and supports* ***[goal: muscle gain, weight loss, general health]****?"*

4. Summarize a Topic

"Can you summarize ***[topic]*** *in* ***[word limit]*** *words while covering the most important points?"*

5. Write a Persuasive Argument

"Can you write a ***[length]*** *persuasive argument on* ***[topic]****, focusing on* ***[specific viewpoint]*** *and including* ***[key points]****?"*

6. Create a Workout Plan

"Can you design a ***[duration]-week*** *workout plan for* ***[fitness goal: muscle gain, fat loss, endurance]****, considering* ***[specific conditions: home gym, limited equipment, etc.]****?"*

7. Provide Step-by-Step Instructions

"Can you give me step-by-step instructions on ***[task]****, assuming I have* ***[beginner/intermediate/advanced]*** *experience?"*

8. Generate Business Ideas

"Can you suggest ***[number]*** *profitable business ideas related to* ***[industry/niche]****, requiring* ***[budget: low, medium, high]*** *startup costs?"*

9. Code Assistance

*"Can you help me debug this **[programming language]** code that is supposed to **[expected behavior]** but is instead **[issue/error]**?"*

10. Craft an Email or Message

*"Can you draft a **[formal/casual]** email to **[recipient]** about **[topic]**, ensuring it is **[tone: professional, apologetic, persuasive, etc.]**?"*

11. Generate a Story Idea

*"Can you provide a unique story idea in the **[genre]** genre, featuring a **[character type]** who must **[main conflict]**?"*

12. Improve Writing

*"Can you revise this sentence/paragraph for better clarity and impact: **[insert text]**?"*

13. Fact-Check Information

*"Can you fact-check this statement: **[insert claim]**, and provide sources if possible?"*

14. Brainstorm Social Media Content

*"Can you suggest **[number]** engaging post ideas for **[platform]** that cater to **[target audience]** in **[niche/industry]**?"*

15. Recommend a Product or Service

*"What is the best **[product/service]** for **[specific need]**, considering **[budget: low, medium, high]** and **[specific preferences]**?"*

16. Provide a Troubleshooting Guide

*"Can you help me troubleshoot **[device/software]** that is **[problem]**, and suggest potential fixes?"*

17. Create a Learning Plan

"Can you create a ***[duration]-week*** *learning plan to master* ***[skill/language/topic]****, assuming* ***[beginner/intermediate/advanced]*** *knowledge?"*

18. Generate a Travel Itinerary

"Can you create a ***[number]-day*** *travel itinerary for* ***[destination]****, focusing on* ***[preferences: adventure, relaxation, culture, food]****?"*

19. Suggest Book or Movie Recommendations

"Can you recommend ***[number] [books/movies]*** *similar to* ***[specific book/movie]****, with* ***[specific elements you like: theme, style, characters]****?"*

20. Answer a "What If" Scenario

*"What would happen if **[hypothetical scenario]**, considering *[scientific/historical/logical] perspectives?"*

These **versatile templates** can be customized to fit nearly any request while maintaining clarity and specificity. They are more than just tools—they're a foundational element in your AI toolkit. They empower you to communicate effectively with AI, ensuring that your needs and goals are met with precision. As you become more familiar with using and customizing these templates, you'll find that your interactions with AI become more intuitive and productive. The templates act as a bridge, connecting your intent with the AI's capabilities and opening up new avenues for creativity and innovation. So go ahead, explore these templates, and see how they can elevate your experience with AI.

ITERATING PROMPTS: REFINING FOR BETTER RESULTS

Imagine you're an artist sculpting a masterpiece. Each time you chip away at the stone, you refine the form, bringing it closer to your vision. This iterative process is precisely what happens when refining AI prompts. Prompt iteration involves revising and tweaking your queries to improve the quality of AI responses. It's a cycle of trial, feedback, and improvement. Feedback loops play a crucial role here. They allow you to see what works and what doesn't, offering insights that guide your next move. These loops are about finding errors and spotting opportunities for enhancement, ensuring that each iteration brings you closer to the desired outcome.

Systematic techniques are your best friend when getting started with refining prompts. A/B testing is one of the most straightforward methods. It involves creating two versions of a prompt and comparing their effectiveness. Imagine asking AI to recommend books. You might test the prompt "Suggest books for a rainy day" against "What are some cozy novels for a rainy afternoon?" Analyzing which prompt yields better recommendations helps you understand how subtle changes can impact AI responses. Another approach is scrutinizing the AI's outputs for clues on areas needing refinement. Look for patterns in responses that miss the mark. Are they too vague or perhaps too specific? These observations can guide you in adjusting your prompts for better precision and relevance.

Practice is key to mastering prompt iteration. Start with exercises that focus on refining prompts for customer feedback analysis. Consider a prompt like, "Gather customer opinions about our new product." Refine it by adding context: "Collect detailed feedback from customers who purchased our new eco-friendly product last month." Notice how adding specifics can lead to more targeted and informative responses. Another exercise is to refine prompts based on user satisfaction metrics. Begin with a broad prompt, "Evaluate user satisfaction with our app." Through iteration, narrow it down: "Analyze user satisfaction ratings for the latest app update, focusing on interface usability." By practicing these exercises, you hone your skills in crafting prompts that yield actionable insights and meaningful results.

The benefits of iterative refinement in prompt engineering are substantial. With each round of refinement, prompts become more accurate and relevant, leading to AI outputs that closely align with your expectations. This precision not only enhances efficiency but also boosts user satisfaction and engagement. Users are more likely to interact positively with AI systems that consistently deliver helpful and precise results. The iterative process also fosters a deeper understanding of how AI interprets prompts, allowing you to anticipate and address potential issues before they arise. As prompts improve, they become powerful tools that maximize the potential of AI, transforming it from a simple responder into a proactive partner in achieving your goals.

STACKING PROMPTS: TECHNIQUES FOR ENHANCED OUTPUT

Imagine trying to solve a puzzle with just one piece. It wouldn't make much sense, right? That's where the concept of stacking prompts comes into play, transforming AI interactions into a more coherent and dynamic experience. Stacking prompts involves creating a series of interconnected queries that guide an AI through complex tasks, much like building a multi-story structure one floor at a time. This technique allows for sequential prompts, where each step builds upon the last, ensuring the AI tackles each phase of a task methodically. Think about planning a project: you wouldn't jump straight to the execution phase without first outlining your objectives and resources. Similarly, when stacking prompts, each layer serves a distinct purpose, contributing to a detailed and nuanced response that a single prompt alone couldn't achieve.

The benefits of stacking prompts are manifold, mainly when dealing with intricate or multifaceted tasks. By layering prompts, you guide the AI to retrieve detailed information, yielding comprehensive outputs that are both nuanced and precise. This approach streamlines workflows, breaking down complex processes into manageable segments and allowing the AI to address each aspect thoroughly. Whether you're coordinating a project or developing a detailed report, stacking prompts provide a structured pathway for the AI to follow, reducing the risk of oversight and enhancing the quality of the final output. This method is like having a checklist for a complicated task. Each item ensures nothing is forgotten, resulting in a thorough and well-rounded result.

To practice stacking techniques, consider exercises that challenge you to design multi-step interactions. For instance, when managing a project, try crafting a series of prompts that cover the planning, execution, and evaluation phases. Begin with a prompt to outline project goals, followed by one to allocate resources, and a final prompt to assess progress.

Example of a Series of Stacked Prompts for Project Management

This sequence of prompts guides the user through **the planning, execution, and evaluation** of a project, ensuring clarity and depth at each stage.

Step 1: Project Planning – Defining Goals and Objectives

Prompt:

*"Can you help me outline a project plan for **[project name]**, which aims to achieve **[specific goal]** within **[timeframe]**? The plan should include key milestones, deliverables, and potential risks."*

➡ *This establishes the foundation, ensuring a clear direction before moving forward.*

Step 2: Resource Allocation and Team Assignments

Prompt:

"Based on the project plan for ***[project name]****, can you suggest an optimal allocation of resources, including personnel, budget, and tools? Also, outline the roles and responsibilities of key team members."*

➡️ *This ensures that necessary resources are assigned efficiently and every team member knows their role.*

Step 3: Execution – Creating an Actionable Timeline

Prompt:

"Can you break down the project timeline into actionable weekly tasks, ensuring a smooth workflow and tracking dependencies? Highlight potential bottlenecks and suggest ways to mitigate them."

➡️ *This step translates the plan into concrete actions with a structured timeline.*

Step 4: Progress Tracking and Issue Resolution

Prompt:

"What are the best methods to monitor the progress of ***[project name]*** *and identify issues early? Can you suggest tracking tools, key performance indicators (KPIs), and a reporting structure for regular updates?"*

➡️ *This introduces a system for accountability and continuous improvement during execution.*

Step 5: Post-Project Evaluation and Lessons Learned

Prompt:

"Now that the project is completed, can you provide a structured framework for evaluating its success? Include a way to measure outcomes against initial goals, gather stakeholder feedback, and document lessons learned for future projects."

This ensures that insights from the project are captured and improvements can be made for future endeavors.

This stacked prompt approach systematically guides the project from concept to completion, ensuring each step builds upon the previous one for a seamless workflow.

Another exercise might involve generating a detailed report, where prompts guide the AI through data collection, analysis, and presentation.

Example of a Series of Stacked Prompts for Generating a Detailed Report

This sequence of prompts systematically guides the AI through data collection, analysis, and presentation to create a comprehensive report.

Step 1: Define the Scope of the Report

Prompt:

*"I need a detailed report on **[topic]**. Can you outline the key sections that should be included, ensuring they cover **[specific aspects, e.g., trends, statistics, case studies]**?"*

This helps define the structure before diving into data collection.

Step 2: Data Collection – Gathering Key Facts and Figures

Prompt:

*"Can you collect the most recent and relevant data on **[specific topic]**, including statistics, industry trends, and expert insights? Provide sources where possible."*

This ensures the report is data-driven and credible.

Step 3: Data Analysis – Identifying Key Patterns and Insights

Prompt:

"Based on the collected data, can you analyze the key trends, patterns, and correlations? Summarize the most important findings and highlight any unexpected insights."

➡️ *This step extracts meaning from raw data and organizes it into valuable takeaways.*

Step 4: Structuring the Report into a Coherent Narrative

Prompt:

"Can you organize the findings into a clear and structured report, ensuring each section has a concise summary and key takeaways? The format should include ***[e.g., introduction, data analysis, key insights, recommendations, conclusion]****."*

➡️ *This ensures the information flows logically and is easy to follow.*

Step 5: Presentation – Formatting for Readability and Impact

Prompt:

"Can you refine the report for clarity and readability by summarizing key points in bullet points, adding headings, and suggesting visuals such as charts or graphs where applicable?"

➡️ *This enhances the readability and impact of the report.*

Step 6: Final Review and Executive Summary

Prompt:

"Can you generate an executive summary that captures the most important findings and recommendations from the report in ***[word count]*** *words? This should be concise but informative."*

➡️ *This provides a high-level summary for decision-makers who may not read the full report.*

This stacked prompt approach moves logically from data collection → analysis → structured writing → presentation, ensuring a high-quality, well-structured, and actionable report.

By practicing these exercises, you refine your ability to craft effective stacked prompts, enhancing your problem-solving skills and understanding of leveraging AI for complex tasks.

In the professional world, stacking prompts can revolutionize decision-making processes. Consider an AI-assisted decision-making application, where layered prompts help the AI sift through data, identify trends, and offer recommendations. This structured approach speeds up the decision-making process and improves accuracy by ensuring all relevant information is considered. In creative settings, stacking prompts can assist in developing interactive applications. For example, imagine a game where player inputs guide the storyline. Stacked prompts can help the AI adapt the narrative based on player choices, creating a dynamic and engaging experience. These real-world applications highlight the versatility of stacking prompts, demonstrating their potential to transform both professional and creative endeavors.

As we wrap up this chapter, remember that stacking prompts offers a powerful way to enhance your interactions with AI, providing a structured and methodical approach to complex tasks. This technique, along with the others we've explored, equips you with the tools to communicate effectively with AI, maximizing its potential in various applications. As we move forward, we'll explore how these skills can be applied in the workplace, unlocking new levels of productivity and creativity.

4
BUILDING YOUR PERSONAL AI ASSISTANT

Imagine waking up each day to an assistant that knows your schedule, anticipates your needs, and even suggests the perfect time for a yoga break. This isn't a distant fantasy—it's the potential of a personal AI assistant tailored just for you. Creating your own AI assistant starts with defining its purpose and scope. This is where you'll decide what functions your assistant will perform, whether it's managing your calendar, sending you reminders, or even playing your favorite music playlist. Think about your daily routine. What tasks could be automated to save you time? Personal scheduling is a common function, along with setting reminders for important meetings or deadlines. But the beauty of a personal AI assistant is its ability to be tailored to your specific needs, whether personal or professional.

CHOOSING THE RIGHT TOOLS: PLATFORMS AND SOFTWARE

When building your personal AI assistant, choosing the right tools is crucial. You have a plethora of platforms and software options at your fingertips. Each has unique strengths and can be tailored to fit your needs. Let's start with the big names you might already know: OpenAI ChatGPT, Google Gemini, Amazon Alexa, and Microsoft Copilot. OpenAI has recently released its new model ChatGPT-4o with Scheduled Tasks, allowing users to automate ChatGPT interactions at predefined times, useful for daily planning and scheduling reminders. Google Gemini is great if you're already integrated into Google's ecosystem. It's known for its robust natural language processing and seamless integration with Google services. Amazon Alexa, on the other hand, is a powerhouse for smart home devices. It offers a range of skills and is highly customizable. Microsoft Copilot, though less popular, is a solid choice for those who rely heavily on Windows and Microsoft's suite of applications. Each platform offers distinct advantages, so your choice might depend on the tech ecosystem you're most comfortable with.

If customization is your priority, open-source platforms like OpenVoiceOS are worth considering. OpenVoiceOS is an excellent choice for those who want to tweak their AI assistant to perform specific tasks. It allows you to modify its functionalities according to your specific needs, without being tied to a particular brand. This can be particularly useful if you have unique requirements or want to experiment with AI technology in a more hands-on way. The open-source nature means you can collaborate with a community of developers, sharing insights and improvements to enhance the platform's capabilities. OpenVoiceOS is ideal if you're tech-savvy and keen on having more control over your AI assistant's behavior and features.

Integration and compatibility are factors you cannot overlook. Your AI assistant should work effortlessly with the devices and applications you use daily. Whether it's your smartphone, computer, or smart home gadgets, seamless compatibility ensures a smooth experience. Imagine asking your assistant to play music on your smart speaker or to sync with your fitness tracker. These interactions should feel natural and intuitive. If you're using a platform like

Google Gemini, you can expect excellent integration with Android devices, while Amazon Alexa excels in environments with multiple smart home devices. Ensuring compatibility means you can maximize the potential of your AI assistant without running into frustrating technical barriers.

For those interested in building a highly customized AI assistant, software development kits (SDKs) are your best friends. SDKs provide the tools and resources to develop and refine your assistant's capabilities. Take the Alexa Skills Kit, for instance. It allows developers to create new skills for Alexa, expanding its functionalities beyond what's available out-of-the-box. This means you can tailor Alexa to perform tasks specific to your lifestyle or business needs. Integrating SDKs into your development process involves setting up an environment where you can test and deploy new features. It might require some coding knowledge, but the result is a personalized AI assistant that aligns perfectly with your requirements.

Cost and accessibility are essential to consider when choosing your platform and tools. Some platforms offer free versions with basic functionalities, while others might require a subscription for advanced features. Free options provide a great starting point for beginners who want to explore AI without a financial commitment. However, paid options offer enhanced capabilities, better support, and frequent updates. Accessibility is another factor—make sure your chosen platform is user-friendly and accommodates your technical skill level. Whether you're a novice exploring AI for the first time or an experienced developer seeking a deep dive, there's a platform out there that fits your needs.

STEP-BY-STEP EXERCISE: BUILDING YOUR EMAIL MANAGER AI ASSISTANT

Imagine you're about to cook a new dish. Your recipe, ingredients, and tools are laid out and ready for action. Building your AI assistant is somewhat similar, requiring a mix of preparation, execution, and a dash of creativity.

As previously mentioned, Gemini is automatically integrated into the Google ecosystem, so it can access most Google apps and perform various tasks for you, like summarizing unread emails in your inbox and adding events to your Google calendar. But it doesn't perform automated tasks. It needs a prompt to trigger an action. OpenAI's new model ChatGPT-4o with Scheduled Tasks can perform basic automations like sending reminders but can't automatically access other apps. Both of these out-of-the-box assistants are useful but fall short of true automation. In the following exercise, we will connect ChatGPT to our Gmail and train it to automatically summarize new emails in our inbox and send them as a push notification to our iPhones using a platform called Make.com. Make is a free platform that allows users to connect apps, create workflows and automate tasks without needing to code. You can integrate 1,000s of apps on this platform, and they provide dozens of templates to get you started creating workflows and automations.

As it happens Make offers a template enabling ChatGPT to summarize emails and send them to your Apple device via push notifications. Follow the set-up guide they provide, and you'll be good to go. To set up this automation manually and work through the exercise, follow along with the step by step guide below.

Step 1: Set Up a free Make.com Account

1. **Sign up** or **log in** to Make.com.
2. Click **"Create a new scenario."**

Step 2: Add the Gmail Trigger

1. Click the big **"+"** button to add a module.
2. Search for **Gmail** and select it.
3. Choose **"Watch Emails"** as the trigger.

4. Click **Add** to connect your Gmail account. Connecting your Gmail account for the first time requires providing an API key. Make will guide you through this process step by step.
5. Set up the trigger options:
   - **Folder:** Inbox (or specific folder).
   - **Criteria:** Only Unread emails
   - **Mark As Read:** Choose if emails are marked as read after processing.
   - **Limit:** Set how many emails to process per cycle.

STEP 3: ADD OPENAI (CHATGPT) FOR SUMMARIZATION

1. Click the **"+"** button after the Gmail module.
2. Search for **OpenAI (ChatGPT)** and select it.
3. Choose **"ChatGPT (GPT-4) - Create a Chat Completion"**.
4. Click **Add** to connect your OpenAI API key.
   - If you don't have an API key, get one from OpenAI's API page.
5. **Set up the request: (refer to image below)**
   - **Model:** chatgpt-4o-latest (system)(or gpt-3.5-turbo if you want a cheaper option).
   - **Role:** User (drop down under **Messages)**
   - **Text Content:**
   - Summarize the following email briefly:
   - Sender: Sender: Sender name
   - Subject: Subject
   - Body: Text content
   - **Temperature:** 0.3 (keeps responses factual).
   - **Max Tokens:** 100-200 (short summary).

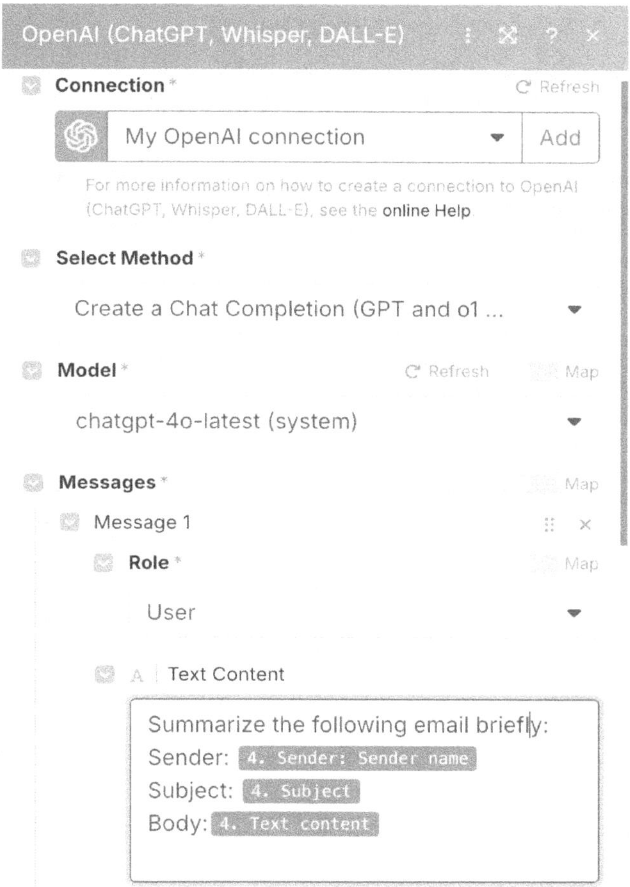

STEP 4: ADD PUSH NOTIFICATION TO YOUR IPHONE WITH APPLE IOS

1. Click the **"+"** button after ChatGPT.
2. Search for **Apple iOS** and select **"Send a Push Notification."**
3. Connect your **Apple device** account.
4. Set up: (refer to image below)
    - **Device:** Your iPhone
    - **Title:** Subject
    - **Body:**

- Sender: Sender: Sender name
- Email: Sender: Email address
- Summary: Choices [ ] : Message.Content

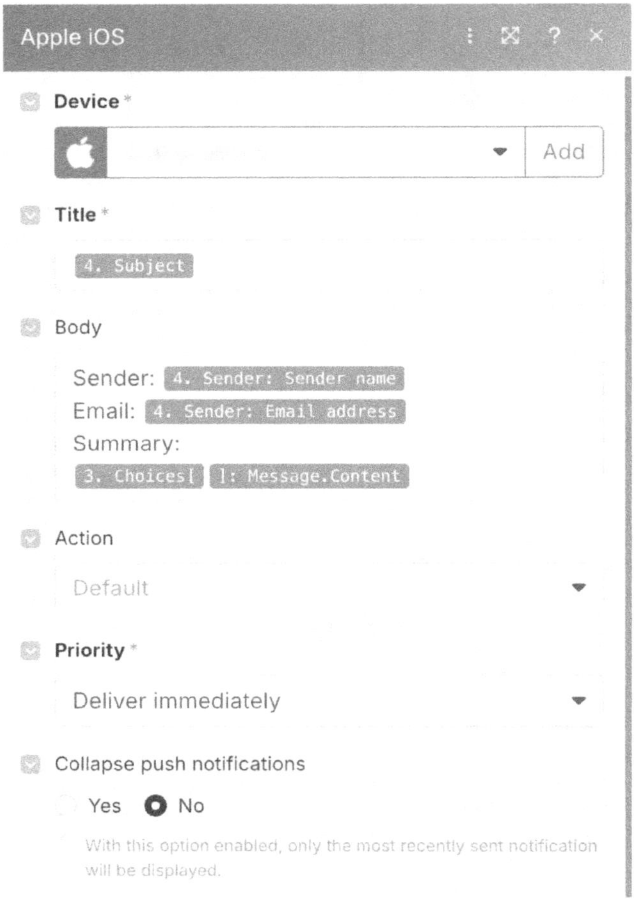

This simple automation is a nice first step towards leveraging the power of AI to help simplify and organize mundane tasks. It is also a good introduction to integrating apps with a third-party platform. Think about taking it a step further and creating another automation to have ChatGPT respond to new emails and save them to your Drafts folder for your review before sending.

SYNCING AI ASSISTANT WITH YOUR CALENDAR: STREAMLINING YOUR SCHEDULE

Imagine beginning your day with a gentle nudge from your AI assistant, reminding you of your morning meeting while seamlessly adjusting your schedule to fit in a quick gym session. This isn't just a dream—it's the practical reality of syncing your AI assistant with your calendar. Integrating these two powerful tools can significantly enhance productivity and organization. Real-time scheduling and reminder features ensure you never miss a beat, whether it's a last-minute meeting or a birthday reminder. Your AI assistant can automate task management, prioritizing what's urgent while allowing flexibility. This automation allows you to focus on what truly matters as your assistant handles the intricacies of your daily agenda.

Imagine a weekly team meeting automatically added every Monday at 10 AM, freeing you from the repetitive task of manual entry. This synchronization ensures that your AI assistant has the most up-to-date information, enabling it to provide timely alerts and reminders that keep you on track.

Advanced scheduling features take this integration to the next level, offering intelligent conflict detection and resolution. Picture your assistant spotting a double-booked afternoon and suggesting alternative times that fit seamlessly into your schedule. This capability reduces the stress of managing overlapping commitments, allowing you to maintain a balanced schedule. Moreover, your AI assistant can offer suggestions for optimizing your daily routine. Maybe it notices you have energy dips in the afternoon and recommends scheduling critical tasks in the morning. Or perhaps it suggests blocking time for focused work, minimizing distractions and maximizing productivity. These insights transform your calendar from a static tool into a dynamic partner in productivity, tailored to your unique preferences and habits.

Integrating your AI assistant with your calendar is about more than convenience—it's about transforming how you manage your time and tasks.

Several highly rated AI scheduling assistants on the market integrate with popular calendar services like Google Calendar, Microsoft Outlook, or Apple Calendar. A few of the best options include: **Reclaim**, an excellent tool for protecting your habits and managing recurring events. **SkedPal** incorporates a highly effective time budgeting feature. **Katch** is an AI scheduling assistant where most scheduling occurs in your inbox. **Trevor** is a free AI solution that is intuitive and has simple controls for scheduling and managing tasks.

These AI powered scheduling tools typically have a free plan with an option for a paid subscription to access their full capabilities. This integration process is straightforward, akin to adding a new app to your smartphone. First, you'll access your calendar settings and look for integration options, usually found in the 'add-ons' or 'extensions' section. Here, you'll find prompts to connect your AI assistant, often requiring you to grant permissions to access your calendar data. Once connected, setting up recurring events and reminders becomes a breeze.

Another option to manually build an AI calender assistant is to integrate ChatGPT to your email account with Make.com. This integration is more complex than syncing ChatGPT to your email and beyond the scope of this book. On the flip side, if you use Google Calendar, a simple alternative is to use Gemini to manage your tasks and calendar events.

As you explore these possibilities, consider how they can be tailored to fit your lifestyle and professional needs, creating a personalized scheduling experience that supports your goals and aspirations.

UPLOADING DOCUMENTS FOR ANALYSIS: AI BEYOND TEXT

Imagine having a stack of business reports or academic papers and needing to pull out key insights quickly. This is where AI assistants shine, offering capabilities beyond simple text interaction. AI can now analyze and summarize documents, transforming how we handle information. Think about the hours you could save by letting an AI sift through dense reports or lengthy research papers, highlighting essential points and summarizing them into manageable chunks. Whether you're a business executive needing insights from financial reports or a student wanting a summary of complex academic articles, AI-driven document analysis can be a game-changer. It offers a level of efficiency that allows you to focus on decision-making and strategy rather than getting bogged down in details. The magic happens when you configure your AI to extract key information and insights. You can set parameters for what you're looking for, whether it's financial data, trends, or specific keywords. This configuration transforms your AI into an analytical powerhouse, providing tailored insights based on your unique needs.

The practical applications of AI-driven document analysis are vast and varied. In the legal field, for example, AI can assist with document review and contract analysis, identifying potential issues or clauses that require attention. Imagine the time saved by having your AI highlight areas in a contract that deviate from standard terms. In academic research, AI can support scientists by summarizing vast amounts of literature, allowing researchers to stay informed without being overwhelmed. This support extends to many fields, from marketing, where AI can analyze consumer feedback and trends, to healthcare, where patient data can be reviewed efficiently. The possibilities are endless, each one enhancing productivity and enabling professionals to focus on higher-level tasks.

However, AI document analysis has challenges and limitations like any advanced technology. One of the primary issues is handling diverse document formats. While AI can be trained to recognize and process different types of files, ensuring compatibility across all formats can be complex. It's like trying to fit a square peg into a round hole—some formats might require additional configuration or conversion before analysis. Ensuring accuracy in extracting complex information is another challenge. AI is incredibly powerful, but it isn't infallible. It can struggle with nuanced language or context, leading to potential misinterpretations. This is why verifying AI-generated insights is essential, especially when they form the basis for critical decisions. Regular updates and training can help improve accuracy, but human oversight remains necessary to ensure reliability.

Despite these challenges, the benefits of AI document analysis are undeniable. It represents a significant step forward in how we interact with information, offering speed, efficiency, and insights that were once beyond reach. Incorporating these capabilities into your AI assistant opens up new avenues for productivity and innovation, transforming how you approach routine tasks and complex projects.

PRACTICAL APPLICATIONS OF YOUR AI ASSISTANT: REAL-WORLD INTEGRATION

Imagine walking into your home, and with a simple command, your AI assistant dims the lights, adjusts the thermostat, and plays your favorite playlist. This is one of the many ways a personal AI assistant can seamlessly integrate into your daily life. Home automation is a growing field where AI assistants thrive, offering control over various smart devices, from lights to security systems. Imagine setting a bedtime routine where the assistant locks doors, turns off unnecessary lights, and sets your alarm for the morning. Beyond convenience, this integration can lead to energy savings and enhanced security, making your home smarter and more efficient.

In personal finance management, AI assistants can be a game-changer. Picture having a financial advisor at your fingertips, ready to track your spending habits, remind you of upcoming bills, and even suggest budget adjustments. Access to your financial data allows an AI assistant to analyze trends and provide insights into your spending patterns. It can help you set savings goals and alert you when you're close to reaching them. This kind of proactive assistance takes the stress out of managing finances, allowing you to focus on achieving your financial objectives. By integrating with your bank accounts and financial apps, your assistant becomes a central hub for your financial management needs.

In professional settings, the applications of AI assistants are vast and varied. For example, AI can assist with patient monitoring and appointment scheduling in healthcare. Imagine a system that tracks vital signs and alerts medical staff to anomalies, ensuring timely intervention. It can also manage patient appointments, reducing the administrative burden on healthcare providers. Similarly, in education, AI assistants can offer personalized learning experiences. Picture a virtual tutor that adapts to each student's learning pace, providing customized lessons and feedback. This level of personalization enhances the educational experience, making learning more engaging and effective.

Customization is key to unlocking the full potential of your AI assistant. You can tailor its functionalities by integrating third-party services and applications to meet unique user requirements. Whether connecting to a specific CRM for business needs or syncing with a fitness tracker for health goals, the ability to customize interactions sets your assistant apart. Personalizing based on user habits and preferences ensures that every interaction feels natural and intuitive. This could mean adjusting the assistant's tone to match your communication style or setting it to prioritize tasks that align with your daily routine.

Looking ahead, the future expansion possibilities for AI assistants are exciting. As new technologies emerge, your assistant can incorporate updates to remain cutting-edge. Imagine integrating natural language processing or machine learning advancements to enhance its capabilities. Expanding functionalities to accommodate evolving user needs ensures your assistant grows alongside you. Whether it's adapting to changes in your lifestyle or embracing new tech trends, the growth potential is limitless. This adaptability means your assistant remains a relevant and valuable tool, ready to tackle whatever challenges or opportunities come your way.

By now, you should have a solid understanding of how AI assistants can transform personal and professional life aspects. The possibilities are vast, from managing home devices to revolutionizing education and healthcare. As developments continue, integrating AI into everyday scenarios will become even more seamless, leading us into a world where personalized, intelligent assistance is the norm. Next, we'll explore how AI can be leveraged in professional environments to boost productivity, enhance creativity, and drive innovation.

MAKE A DIFFERENCE WITH YOUR REVIEW

UNLOCK THE POWER OF GENEROSITY

> *"Some people call this artificial intelligence, but the reality is this technology will enhance us. So instead of artificial intelligence, I think we'll augment our intelligence."*
>
> — GINNI ROMETTY, FORMER CEO OF IBM

Did you know that when you help others, you actually make **your own life better**? It's true! So let's make something great happen — together.

Would you help someone just like you—curious about AI and ChatGPT but not sure where to start?

My mission is simple: **make AI easy, fun, and useful for everyone** — no confusing tech talk. Just real-life ways to use AI to boost creativity, save time, and make life better.

But to reach more people who need this, I need your help.

Here's the deal: **Most people pick books based on reviews.** So when you leave a review, you're not just helping me — **you're helping someone else get started with AI too!**

Think about it. Your review could help:

- One more small business owner grow their dream.
- One more creative person finally write that book or launch that project.
- One more busy parent use AI to save time and stress less.
- One more employee get ahead at work.
- One more person discover how AI can make life easier.

It takes less than a minute and costs nothing — but it could make a huge difference.

Just scan the QR code or visit this link to leave a review:

[https://www.amazon.com/review/review-your-purchases/?asin=BOOKASIN]

If you love helping others, **you're my kind of person**.

Thank you so much — it truly means the world to me!

— Kai Sinclair

5
AI IN THE WORKPLACE

Imagine walking into your office and finding that your tasks have already been organized for the day. Your emails are sorted, meetings planned, and reminders set—all before you've had your first cup of coffee. This isn't just wishful thinking; it's the power of AI transforming the workplace into a well-oiled machine. With AI, you can streamline tasks and boost productivity, making your workday not only more efficient but also more enjoyable. AI is reshaping how we manage tasks and workflows, helping us focus on what truly matters.

At the heart of AI-driven productivity is task management, where AI tools optimize how you prioritize and schedule your day. Think of project management software like Asana, which integrates AI to help you stay on top of deadlines and team activities. These tools ensure you never miss a beat, sending automated reminders and tracking deadlines so you can focus on more critical tasks. Imagine a virtual assistant that reminds you of every meeting, freeing you from the stress of juggling schedules. This kind of automation keeps everything running smoothly, ensuring you have time to focus on what requires your unique skills and attention.

AI isn't just about keeping track of tasks; it's about making processes more efficient. Workflow automation handles repetitive, mundane tasks, reducing errors and saving time. Consider document processing, where AI uses Optical Character Recognition (OCR) to automate data entry from scanned documents. This technology eliminates manual data input, ensuring accuracy and freeing up your time for more complex activities. Similarly, AI algorithms can filter and prioritize emails, sorting urgent messages from spam so you can tackle your inbox with ease. It's like having an extra pair of hands, always ready to handle the repetitive tasks that used to slow you down.

One of AI's most powerful features is its ability to provide real-time insights, enabling quicker and more informed decision-making. Imagine having a dashboard displaying project updates as they happen, offering a clear view of progress and potential roadblocks. These AI dashboards translate data into actionable insights, helping you make decisions based on real-time information. Whether adjusting timelines or reallocating resources, AI ensures you're always a step ahead, making decisions with confidence and clarity. This capability transforms your role from reactive to proactive, allowing you to steer projects toward success.

AI tools also enhance productivity metrics, offering a transparent view of performance across teams and projects. You gain a deeper understanding of efficiency and output through AI-generated analytics and reports. These insights help identify areas for improvement, guiding you in optimizing workflows and boosting productivity. Imagine having a report that tells you how your team is performing and where bottlenecks are occurring. With this data, you can make adjustments that enhance overall productivity, ensuring everyone is working at their best. AI doesn't just measure success—it helps you achieve it.

Interactive Element: Try It Out!

Create a list of tasks you manage daily. Identify which tasks could benefit from AI-driven automation or optimization. Consider tools you could use to streamline these tasks: automating email sorting, setting up reminders, or using AI-powered project management software. Reflect on how these changes could impact your productivity and work-life balance. Write down your thoughts and plan a strategy to implement these AI tools in your daily routine.

CREATIVE PROBLEM SOLVING WITH AI: INNOVATING SOLUTIONS

Imagine sitting around a table with your team, brainstorming the next big product. Everyone throws ideas around, but nothing seems to stick. Enter AI brainstorming tools—your new creative partner. These tools act like a fresh set of eyes, capable of processing vast amounts of information to suggest innovative ideas you might never have considered. They're not just about generating ideas; they help refine them, turning vague concepts into actionable plans. It's like having endless creativity at your fingertips, ready to help you develop the next groundbreaking product. If you want to boost your creative process with AI assistance, here are a few applications to consider. **Ideamap** offers built-in AI tools to analyze ideas, generate inspiration, visualize concepts, detect topics, and identify duplicates. If you are working with a team, **MindMeister** is an online mind-mapping application that allows users to visualize, share, and present their thoughts via the cloud, facilitating real-time collaboration and idea generation. **Miro** is an online whiteboard that allows you to brainstorm ideas, outline strategy, and edit text. **Coggle** is a tool that will enable you to build sophisticated mind maps.

In creative industries, generative design software also plays a crucial role. Think of it as a digital collaborator that enables you to design everything from fashion to architecture. This software can explore countless design variations, optimizing them based on your criteria, whether it's aesthetics, functionality, or sustainability. We've already explored platforms like Midjourney, DALL-E, and Firefly. Still, there are many other fascinating AI design tools worth considering. **Pixlr** is a cloud-based image editing suite with AI-powered tools for simple and advanced photo editing, offering image generation and enhancement features. **Stable Diffusion**, a deep learning text-to-image model, creates highly detailed images from textual descriptions and supports advanced applications such as inpainting, outpainting, and image-to-image translation. Meanwhile, **Framer** simplifies web design by allowing users to describe the website they envision—the platform then generates it, enabling seamless editing and instant publishing.

In research and development, AI is proving to be a game-changer. Take drug discovery, for instance. AI simulations can process and analyze biological data at speeds humans can't match, identifying potential drug candidates in a fraction of the time. This acceleration speeds up the R&D process and reduces costs, making the discovery of life-saving drugs more feasible. Similarly, AI helps discover new materials with unique properties in materials science and engineering. By analyzing vast datasets, AI can predict how different materials will interact, driving innovation in fields like aerospace and electronics. It's like having a supercomputer dedicated to solving the toughest challenges in science and engineering, opening doors to discoveries that were once out of reach.

Real-world examples of AI innovation showcase its transformative power. Consider sustainable energy solutions. AI analyzes weather patterns and energy consumption data to optimize the use of renewable resources, significantly improving efficiency and reducing waste. In smart city planning, AI data analytics are used to design urban spaces that are more efficient, sustainable, and responsive to the needs of residents. This technology can optimize traffic flow, reduce pollution, and enhance the quality of life for city dwellers.

These examples demonstrate AI's potential to address some of the world's most pressing challenges, offering innovative solutions that impact our lives daily.

AI isn't just a tool—it's a creative partner. When humans and AI collaborate, the possibilities are endless. Imagine co-creating art installations where AI-generated inputs blend with human creativity, producing pieces that challenge the boundaries of traditional art. In writing and storytelling, AI can assist in developing plotlines or characters, providing fresh perspectives that fuel creativity. Workshops where writers and AI work together are becoming more common, offering a new approach to storytelling that combines human intuition with AI's analytical capabilities. This cohesion between human imagination and AI's computational power can lead to novel concepts and solutions, pushing the boundaries of what's possible in the creative realm.

ENHANCING COLLABORATION: AI IN TEAM DYNAMICS

Picture a team scattered across continents, each member speaking a different language. Yet, they communicate effortlessly, like they were in the same room. This is the magic of AI-powered translation services, which break down language barriers and allow global teams to collaborate seamlessly. These tools ensure that everyone is on the same page, regardless of their native tongue, making communication not just possible but effective. Imagine the potential for creativity and innovation when ideas flow freely across borders. AI doesn't stop at translation. During meetings, real-time transcription tools capture every word, providing instant notes that can be shared with those who couldn't attend. It's like having a personal scribe, ensuring nothing gets lost in conversation.

Collaboration is more than just communication. It's about working together efficiently, and AI plays a pivotal role here. Think about version control and document sharing. AI-enhanced platforms ensure everyone can access the latest document versions, reducing confusion and errors. There's no more "Is this the right file?" panic. With AI-driven task allocation and resource management, teams can function like a well-tuned orchestra, with each member knowing their role and available resources. It's a system that adapts to change, reallocating tasks as priorities shift, ensuring that no one is overburdened and that deadlines are easily met. This coordination allows teams to focus on what they do best—innovate and create.

In today's world, where remote and hybrid work environments are becoming the norm, virtual collaboration tools backed by AI are indispensable. Virtual meeting assistants such as **Fireflies.AI, Zoom AI Companion,** and **MeetGeek** schedule and coordinate meetings and suggest optimal times based on everyone's availability. Gone are the days of endless email threads trying to pin down a meeting slot. AI-enhanced virtual workspaces provide a platform where team interactions are fluid and natural. These spaces allow for brainstorming sessions, team huddles, and even casual coffee chats, all from the comfort of your home office. It's about creating a sense of presence and connection, no matter where you are, bridging the gap between remote colleagues, and fostering a sense of unity.

AI's role in team dynamics extends to understanding the human elements of teamwork. Sentiment analysis tools can assess team feedback, providing insights into morale and helping to identify potential conflicts before they escalate. Imagine being able to gauge the mood of your team at a glance, addressing concerns, and boosting morale proactively. AI-driven personality assessments take it a step further, helping align team members based on complementary skills and traits. This understanding can lead to more harmonious teams, where conflicts are minimized, and collaboration flourishes. It's like having a team coach who knows everyone's strengths and weaknesses, guiding them to work together more effectively. This foresight enables teams to function at their highest potential, combining diverse talents into a cohesive unit.

AI FOR DATA ANALYSIS: TURNING INSIGHTS INTO ACTION

Imagine sitting at your desk with mountains of data at your fingertips, and yet, it feels like wading through an endless sea of numbers and charts. Enter AI-powered data analytics, your new best friend in making sense of it all. AI platforms like **Polymer** and **Sisense** can transform raw data into actionable insights that drive decisions and strategies. They use sophisticated algorithms to spot trends and forecast future outcomes, giving you a clearer picture of what's to come. Whether you're in market research, trying to predict consumer behavior, or in finance, anticipating economic shifts, AI's trend analysis capabilities offer a competitive edge. It's like having a crystal ball, but one that's based on complex data and logic.

When it comes to decision support, AI steps up as a reliable ally. Imagine having a dashboard that displays current performance metrics and provides strategic advice based on data-driven insights. These AI dashboards are a staple in business intelligence, allowing you to visualize data intuitively. They make scenario analysis a breeze, helping you easily assess risks and opportunities. Think of it as having a strategic consultant on call, ready to offer insights on demand. By simulating various scenarios, AI helps you weigh different outcomes and make informed decisions, reducing uncertainty and enhancing confidence.

Data visualization is another area where AI shines, turning complex datasets into easy-to-understand visuals. Interactive tools like **Tableau** and **Qlik** allow you to explore data from different angles, revealing patterns that might have gone unnoticed. For instance, AI-generated heatmaps can analyze spatial data, showing where to focus resources or identify problem areas. These visualizations are not just informative; they're engaging, making it easier to communicate findings to others. Imagine presenting your data insights with clarity and impact, ensuring everyone in the room is on the same page.

However, AI data analysis isn't without its challenges. Data accuracy and integrity are crucial, as even the most advanced AI systems can be led astray by poor-quality data. It's like building a house on a shaky foundation—no matter how advanced the tools, the results won't hold up. Data biases are another concern, potentially skewing AI-generated insights. Overcoming these biases requires vigilance and a commitment to using diverse and representative data sets. It's about ensuring that AI decisions are fair and unbiased, reflecting the true picture rather than a distorted one.

As you explore AI-powered data analysis, remember the importance of continuously refining your data inputs and algorithms. This ongoing process helps ensure that the insights you gain are as accurate and valuable as possible. By embracing AI's capabilities while remaining mindful of its limitations, you can unlock a world of new opportunities and drive meaningful change in your organization.

AI-POWERED PROJECT MANAGEMENT: TOOLS AND TIPS

Imagine having a personal assistant who never sleeps and is always ready to keep your projects on track. This is the promise of AI-powered project management tools. These tools take the guesswork out of planning and executing projects by optimizing task prioritization and resource allocation. Picture a tool automatically assessing the workload and assigning tasks based on team members' strengths and availability. This kind of smart allocation ensures that everyone works efficiently, playing to their strengths while maintaining a balanced workload. It's like having a project manager who knows your team inside out, constantly optimizing for the best outcomes.

The benefits of AI in project management are undeniable. Automated progress tracking and reporting let you see exactly where each project stands at a glance, reducing the need for endless status meetings. Imagine a real-time dashboard that shows you which tasks are on track and which need attention. It's not just about knowing where your project stands; it's about spotting potential issues before they become problems. AI-enhanced communication platforms also play a crucial role, facilitating seamless collaboration among team members. With AI-driven tools, it's easier than ever to share updates, documents, and insights, ensuring everyone is aligned and informed.

Choosing the right AI project management tool can seem daunting, but a few key criteria can guide your decision. First, consider the tool's ability to integrate with your existing systems. Compatibility is crucial for smooth implementation without disrupting your current workflows. Look for tools offering customizable features, allowing you to tailor the platform to your needs. Also, consider the learning curve—choose a tool that's intuitive and easy for your team to adopt. When integrating AI into your project frameworks, start small. Implement AI features gradually, allowing your team to acclimate and provide feedback. This iterative approach ensures that the transition is smooth and that the AI truly enhances your workflow. There are dozens of AI-driven project management platforms from which to choose. Here is a list of some of the top AI applications for project management to get you started on your search.

Forecast: This comprehensive AI-powered project management tool handles everything from project initiation to budgeting, resource allocation, and task tracking. It utilizes predictive analysis to project timelines and budget requirements, automating routine tasks and providing real-time insights. With its unified management platform, Forecast streamlines processes, allowing project managers to monitor progress and team productivity without constantly switching between tools.

Taskade: This is an AI-enhanced task management platform designed to streamline tasks, assignments, outlines, checklists, and workflows. It offers real-time collaboration, customizable templates, and AI-powered features that prioritize tasks, set deadlines, and synchronize updates across team members. Its flexibility and customization options make it suitable for managing detailed workflows, boosting task allocation, and enhancing team productivity.

Asana: This versatile project management tool streamlines task management and supports strategic initiatives. It offers features like task assignment, tracking, and project communication enhancements. Integration with tools like Slack and Google Workspace makes Asana a central hub for team activities. Its user-friendly interface and AI features make it an affordable option for small businesses or startups.

ClickUp: This is a versatile, all-in-one project management platform offering advanced task management, built-in time tracking, and agile features like sprint planning and burndown charts. With its customizable interface and extensive integrations, ClickUp adapts to any team's unique needs, making it an excellent choice for diverse workflows.

Clockwise: This AI-powered time management tool optimizes team calendars for enhanced productivity. It adjusts schedules to minimize meeting conflicts and maximize focused work periods, promoting productivity and minimizing disruptions. It's perfect for balancing team collaboration with individual productivity, making it easier to allocate time for important meetings without compromising personal work time.

Keep in mind that AI in project management isn't without its challenges. One common issue is balancing AI automation with human oversight. While automation can streamline processes, it's essential to maintain human oversight to ensure that the AI's decisions align with your strategic goals. Think of AI as a helpful partner, not a replacement for human judgment. Ensuring data integrity and security is another critical concern. With AI systems processing vast amounts of data, safeguarding this information is paramount. Implement robust security measures, such as encryption and access controls, to protect sensitive project data. By addressing these challenges proactively, you can harness the full potential of AI in project management, driving projects forward with efficiency and insight.

AUTOMATING ROUTINE TASKS: AI AS A VIRTUAL ASSISTANT

Imagine waking up and knowing all your mundane tasks are already sorted out. This isn't a distant dream; it's the reality of AI virtual assistants in action. These digital helpers have taken on the role of streamlining everyday tasks, allowing you to focus on what truly matters. Think of AI scheduling assistants—tools that manage your appointments with precision, ensuring you never miss a meeting or deadline. They sync seamlessly with your calendar, juggling appointments with the finesse of a seasoned coordinator. Automated customer service chatbots are another marvel, handling inquiries around the clock efficiently and consistently. They provide instant responses, resolve common issues, and enable human agents to tackle more complex problems.

The benefits of automating these routine tasks are numerous. One significant advantage is the reduction of human error. AI ensures accuracy in data entry and processing, minimizing mistakes that can lead to costly consequences. Consider the tedious task of updating spreadsheets; AI can handle this with precision, leaving no room for error. This automation translates to increased efficiency, especially in administrative roles where repetitive tasks are the norm. Routine tasks that once consumed valuable time are now completed swiftly, allowing you to dedicate your efforts to more strategic and creative endeavors. It's like having a personal assistant who never tires, always ready to take on the tasks you'd rather avoid.

AI virtual assistants have made their mark across various industries, tailoring their capabilities to meet specific needs. AI assists with patient appointment reminders in healthcare, ensuring patients never miss a consultation. This not only enhances patient care but also optimizes scheduling for healthcare providers. Imagine a system automatically adjusting appointment slots based on patient needs and availability, reducing no-shows and maximizing efficiency. In the finance sector, AI takes on the task of automated invoice processing and handling transactions with accuracy and speed. This automation streamlines financial operations, allowing businesses to focus on growth and innovation rather than paperwork. It's a transformation that saves time and resources, making processes more seamless and effective.

Despite these advantages, reliance on AI for task automation isn't without its challenges. Human oversight is crucial to ensure that AI systems align with organizational goals and values. While AI can handle routine tasks, human judgment is indispensable for complex decision-making. It's about balancing automation with the human touch, ensuring that AI serves as an enabler rather than a replacement. Moreover, data privacy and security remain paramount concerns. As AI systems process sensitive information, safeguarding this data is essential to prevent breaches and maintain trust. Implementing robust security measures like encryption and access controls is vital to protect organizational and customer data. This vigilance ensures that AI-driven automation enhances productivity without compromising privacy or security.

ETHICAL CONSIDERATIONS: NAVIGATING AI IN THE WORKPLACE

Incorporating AI into the workplace isn't just about technology; it's deeply intertwined with ethical concerns that demand thoughtful consideration. One major issue is privacy, particularly when AI is used for employee monitoring. Imagine a scenario where AI tracks every move, analyzing productivity and behavior. While this can boost efficiency, it raises questions about surveillance and personal privacy. Employees might feel uneasy knowing their every action is monitored, potentially affecting morale and trust. It's crucial to strike a balance, ensuring AI enhances productivity without infringing on personal freedoms.

Another significant concern is AI's impact on employment. As AI takes on more tasks traditionally performed by humans, there's a growing fear of job displacement. Sectors like manufacturing and administration are particularly vulnerable, where routine tasks are prime candidates for automation. This shift can result in significant job loss, affecting livelihoods and economies. While AI can create new opportunities, such as roles in AI maintenance and development, the transition isn't always smooth. Companies must consider the social implications, investing in retraining programs to help workers adapt to new roles.

Responsible AI practices are key to navigating these challenges. Transparency and accountability in AI decision-making are essential. Employees and stakeholders must understand how AI systems make decisions and their criteria. This openness fosters trust and ensures AI systems align with company values. Additionally, diversity and inclusivity in AI applications are crucial. AI systems should reflect the diversity of the workforce and the communities they serve, avoiding biases that can lead to discrimination. Companies can develop fairer, more equitable AI systems by ensuring diverse data sets and inclusive practices.

Actionable guidelines can help companies implement AI ethically. Developing comprehensive AI policies and frameworks is a start. These guidelines should address privacy, data protection, and the ethical use of AI across the organization. Engaging stakeholders in ethical AI discussions is equally important. Companies can better understand the ethical landscape and make informed decisions by involving employees, customers, and community leaders in the conversation. This collaborative approach ensures AI implementation is aligned with societal values and expectations.

Real-world examples highlight the importance of ethical AI. Some companies prioritize ethical AI in talent acquisition, using AI tools that mitigate bias in hiring processes. By analyzing language and behavior patterns, these tools help create a more diverse and inclusive workforce. Other organizations focus on AI-driven initiatives for social good. For instance, AI systems are used to analyze environmental data, guiding efforts to combat climate change. These initiatives demonstrate how AI can be deployed responsibly, benefiting businesses and society.

As we wrap up our exploration of AI in the workplace, remember that ethical considerations are as vital as technological advancements. We can ensure AI becomes a force for positive change by addressing these challenges with transparency and inclusivity. As we move forward, we'll explore how AI continues to transform industries, driving innovation and shaping the future.

6
AI-POWERED INCOME STREAMS

Imagine waking up to the gentle hum of your smart coffee maker brewing the perfect cup, your AI-powered personal assistant having already synced your schedule with real-time traffic updates, and your smart thermostat adjusting the home temperature based on the weather forecast. This seamless integration of AI into everyday life isn't just about convenience; it's a testament to the transformative potential of AI in business. As AI continues to advance, it opens up many opportunities for businesses to innovate and create value in previously unimaginable ways. Today, organizations of all sizes are exploring how best to harness AI's capabilities to streamline operations and revolutionize their business models, creating new revenue streams and enhancing customer experiences.

When considering AI-driven business models, subscription-based AI services stand out as a game-changer across various industries. Take healthcare, for example. Subscription models allow patients to access AI-powered diagnostic tools that continuously monitor their health. These services provide real-time insights, enabling preventative care and reducing the need for frequent doctor visits. Imagine a service where users pay a monthly fee to access a virtual health assistant that analyzes their medical data and offers personalized health recommendations. Such models improve patient outcomes and create a steady revenue stream for businesses offering these services. Similarly, AI-powered platforms provide on-demand solutions, such as data analysis or content creation, which companies can access as needed without the overhead of maintaining a full-time staff.

AI's role in business transformation is profound. AI enhances efficiency and productivity by optimizing operations, leading to significant cost savings. In supply chain management and logistics, AI-driven systems can predict demand, optimize inventory levels, and streamline delivery routes. Imagine a warehouse where AI monitors stock levels, automatically reorders supplies, and schedules deliveries based on real-time customer demand. This level of automation minimizes waste and ensures products are available when customers need them. In manufacturing, AI-powered predictive maintenance systems analyze machine data to predict when a piece of equipment will fail, allowing for timely repairs and reducing downtime. This proactive approach saves money and extends the machinery's lifespan, providing a competitive edge in the marketplace.

Emerging AI markets present exciting growth opportunities, particularly in personalized medicine and healthcare diagnostics. AI algorithms can analyze vast amounts of patient data to identify patterns and predict health issues before they become critical, revolutionizing how healthcare is delivered. Picture an AI system that analyzes genetic information to tailor treatment plans specific to an individual's unique genetic makeup. This level of personalization enhances treatment efficacy and patient satisfaction. In the realm of smart homes and the Internet of Things (IoT), AI enables devices to learn user preferences and automate daily tasks, creating more efficient and comfortable living environments. Think of a home where the lights, appliances, and security systems all communicate with each other, optimizing energy use and enhancing security based on your habits.

The integration of AI in traditional industries is another area ripe for innovation. In agriculture, AI-powered precision farming can optimize crop yields by analyzing soil conditions, weather patterns, and crop health. Imagine farmers using drones equipped with AI to monitor their fields, providing real-time data that helps them make informed decisions about planting, watering, and harvesting. This technology increases efficiency and sustainability, ensuring food security in the face of a growing global population. In the financial sector, AI-enhanced services offer robo-advisors that provide personalized investment advice based on real-time market data. These advisors analyze investment portfolios, suggest trades, and even execute transactions automatically, democratizing access to financial planning and wealth management.

Reflection: Exploring AI Opportunities in Business

Take a moment to consider how AI can be integrated into your business or profession. Reflect on the areas where AI could streamline processes, enhance customer engagement, or open new revenue streams. Jot down ideas for AI-driven business models that you find intriguing or relevant to your industry. Think about the potential challenges and benefits of adopting these technologies. How might AI reshape your daily operations or alter the landscape of your field? Exploring these questions will help you understand the broader implications of AI in the business world and inspire innovative strategies for leveraging AI to drive success.

AI IN E-COMMERCE: ENHANCING THE CUSTOMER EXPERIENCE

Picture yourself browsing an online store; as you scroll, the website seems to know exactly what you're looking for. This isn't magic; it's AI at work, tailoring your shopping experience to fit your personal preferences. Through AI-driven recommendation engines, online retailers can suggest products based on your past purchases and browsing history. It's like having a personal shopper who knows your style inside and out, suggesting those perfect pair of shoes or the latest gadget you didn't even know you needed. These engines analyze data from countless users to predict what you might like, making shopping more intuitive and enjoyable.

Another fascinating aspect of AI in e-commerce is dynamic pricing, where prices adjust in real-time based on demand, competitor prices, and consumer behavior. Imagine booking a flight and noticing the price fluctuates. That's AI analyzing patterns to offer competitive pricing. This keeps businesses agile and responsive to market changes while ensuring customers get the best deals. For savvy shoppers, understanding these dynamics can lead to more intelligent purchasing decisions. At the same time, it maximizes revenue potential for businesses without alienating customers.

AI doesn't stop at personalizing the shopping experience; it also revolutionizes customer service efficiency. Think of the last time you had a question while shopping online. Instead of waiting on hold, you probably interacted with a chatbot that provided instant answers. These AI-powered chatbots handle inquiries 24/7, offering quick solutions to common problems. They're like the friendly store associate who's always available to help, ensuring customer satisfaction and loyalty. Furthermore, advanced virtual shopping assistants guide purchase decisions, providing tailored advice and product comparisons. This level of service not only enhances the shopping experience but also builds trust, as customers feel valued and understood.

Consider the role of AI in marketing strategies, where it optimizes campaigns by targeting the right audience with the right message. AI analyzes consumer data to identify patterns and predict future behavior, allowing businesses to craft personalized marketing strategies that resonate with individual customers. Imagine receiving an email with product recommendations that align perfectly with your interests. This isn't a coincidence; it's AI-powered email marketing at play, crafting personalized communication that feels less like advertising and more like a helpful suggestion. AI also plays a crucial role in targeted advertising, ensuring that ads appear to those most likely to be interested, thereby increasing conversion rates and maximizing marketing budgets.

Behind the scenes, AI significantly impacts supply chain and inventory management, ensuring that products are available when and where they are needed. By forecasting demand and optimizing inventory levels, AI helps businesses reduce waste and avoid stock-outs. Picture a warehouse where AI systems predict which products will sell most during a particular season, allowing the company to stock up accordingly. This foresight streamlines logistics, ensuring efficient delivery and improved customer satisfaction. AI-powered supply chain management systems can adapt to changing conditions, such as sudden spikes in demand or disruptions in logistics, ensuring seamless operations even in challenging times.

Incorporating AI into e-commerce is not just about staying competitive but redefining the customer experience. By personalizing interactions, streamlining operations, and enhancing service, AI allows businesses to connect with customers in meaningful ways. For consumers, this means a shopping experience that is not only more efficient but also more engaging and enjoyable. With AI, shopping becomes a personalized journey, where each interaction is tailored to the individual's preferences and needs. This level of personalization and efficiency is reshaping the e-commerce landscape, setting new standards for what customers can expect from their online shopping experiences.

AI IN MARKETING: PERSONALIZING CUSTOMER ENGAGEMENT

Imagine receiving a marketing email that seems to speak directly to you, as if it knows your preferences and interests intimately. This is not a coincidence; the magic of AI-driven personalization is at play. AI algorithms have the power to segment audiences with incredible precision, targeting specific groups with tailored messages that resonate deeply. These algorithms analyze vast amounts of data to understand consumer behavior and preferences and predict future actions. By identifying patterns and trends, AI helps marketers create highly personalized campaigns, ensuring that each customer feels like they are the center of attention. Whether it's through personalized product recommendations or custom-tailored advertisements, AI enables businesses to connect with customers on a personal level, fostering loyalty and engagement.

In the realm of digital advertising, real-time personalization is a game-changer. Imagine browsing the web and encountering ads perfectly aligned with your recent searches or purchases. AI makes this possible by adapting ad content in real time based on user interactions. It's like having a personal shopping assistant who knows exactly what you're looking for and presents it to you at the right moment. This level of personalization not only enhances the customer experience but also boosts conversion rates, as consumers are more likely to engage with content that feels relevant and timely. For businesses, this means more effective advertising spend and a greater return on investment.

AI's influence extends beyond personalization to content creation and curation. Picture a world where AI generates captivating blog posts, engaging social media updates, and compelling email newsletters. These AI tools analyze existing content to understand what resonates with audiences and then craft new material that aligns with those insights. It's like having a team of creative writers working around the clock to produce content that captivates and informs. Additionally, AI assists in curating user-generated content, sifting through vast amounts of data to select the most relevant and impactful pieces. This not only saves time but also ensures that the content shared with audiences is of the highest quality and relevance.

Understanding the customer journey is crucial for marketers looking to optimize their strategies, and AI plays a vital role in this process. Predictive analytics provide valuable insights into customer behavior, helping businesses anticipate needs and tailor their offerings accordingly. Imagine a scenario where a business can predict when a customer will likely make a purchase, allowing them to offer targeted promotions at the perfect time. AI also enhances A/B testing, allowing marketers to experiment with different strategies and identify which yield the best results. By analyzing data in real-time, AI helps refine marketing approaches, ensuring that each customer interaction is as effective as possible.

While AI offers numerous benefits, it also raises important ethical considerations that cannot be ignored. Transparency in data collection and use is paramount, as consumers have the right to know how their information is being utilized. Businesses must be upfront about their data practices, ensuring that customers feel informed and secure. Balancing personalization with consumer privacy is another critical challenge. While personalized experiences are valuable, they should not come at the expense of privacy. Ensuring that data is collected and used responsibly, with the customer's consent, is essential for maintaining trust and fostering long-term relationships.

In the ever-evolving landscape of marketing, AI stands as a powerful ally, enabling businesses to engage with customers in ways that were once unimaginable. By leveraging AI-driven personalization techniques, companies can create marketing experiences that are not only effective but also meaningful. As AI continues to advance, the possibilities for enhancing customer engagement are endless, offering exciting opportunities for businesses to innovate and grow.

BUILDING A FREELANCE CAREER WITH AI SKILLS

Imagine working from your cozy home office or a bustling café, using your AI skills to solve complex problems and deliver innovative solutions to clients around the world. As businesses increasingly recognize the value of AI, the demand for skilled freelancers in this field is skyrocketing. You're on the right track if you've been exploring ways to leverage your AI knowledge. Two skills stand out in the freelance market: machine learning model development and data analysis with visualization using AI tools. Machine learning is about creating models to learn from data and make predictions or decisions without being explicitly programmed to perform a task. It's like teaching a computer to recognize patterns and adapt over time. Meanwhile, data analysis and visualization involve interpreting data to uncover meaningful insights and presenting these findings in visually engaging ways. Both skills are essential for helping businesses make data-driven decisions and open doors to a wide range of freelance opportunities.

To thrive as a freelance AI professional, acquiring and honing these skills is crucial. Fortunately, there are plenty of resources available to help you get started. Online platforms offer a variety of AI courses and certifications tailored to different experience levels. Whether you're a complete beginner or looking to deepen your expertise, these courses provide structured learning paths and hands-on projects that prepare you for real-world challenges. **Coursera** offers a variety of AI courses, such as "AI For Everyone" by DeepLearning.AI, which provides a broad understanding that is suitable for business contexts. **IBM SkillsBuild** is a free platform offering courses in AI fundamentals, machine learning, and data analysis, along with recognized digital credentials.

Once you've completed an AI course, you may then be eligible to apply for **The Certified Artificial Intelligence Consultant (CAIC™)** certification program offered by the **United States Artificial Intelligence Institute (USAII®)**. Another certification option is the **Certified Artificial Intelligence Practitioner (CAIP)** certification. Various institutions offer CAIP certifications, including **CertNexus** and the **Global Association for Quality Management (GAQM).** You can enroll in a preparation program to ensure your eligibility for this certification. CertNexus provides its certification program through Coursera.

Participating in AI hackathons and competitions is another excellent way to sharpen your skills. These events bring together AI enthusiasts and professionals to tackle complex problems, offering a collaborative environment where you can learn from others and showcase your abilities. They also provide a platform to experiment with new ideas, pushing your creative and technical boundaries.

Once you're equipped with the necessary skills, it's time to explore freelance platforms where you can find work opportunities. Websites like Upwork, Freelancer and Kolabtree are popular among AI professionals, offering a range of projects that match your expertise and interests. These platforms connect you with clients seeking AI solutions, from startups to established enterprises. Joining AI-specific marketplaces can also boost your visibility. These platforms cater exclusively to tech professionals, increasing your chances of finding projects that align with your skills. Networking in AI and tech communities is equally important. Engaging with like-minded individuals through forums, social media groups, and local meetups can lead to valuable collaborations and referrals. Building a strong professional network expands your reach. It opens doors to exciting projects that might not be advertised on traditional platforms.

Marketing yourself effectively is essential for attracting clients and building a successful freelance career. Start by creating a professional portfolio that showcases your AI projects and highlights your expertise. Include detailed descriptions of your work, illustrating how you've applied your skills to solve real-world problems. This portfolio is a testament to your capabilities, giving potential clients confidence in your ability to deliver results. Leveraging social media and personal branding can further enhance your visibility. Share your insights, achievements, and projects on platforms like LinkedIn, Twitter, and GitHub. Engaging with the online AI community and participating in discussions establishes you as a thought leader, increasing your credibility and attracting clients who value your expertise.

As you navigate the freelance landscape, remember that continuous learning and adaptation are key to staying competitive. AI is a rapidly evolving field, with new tools and techniques emerging regularly. Keep your skills sharp by attending workshops, webinars, and conferences. These events provide opportunities to learn about the latest trends and innovations, ensuring you remain at the forefront of the industry. By staying informed and proactive, you'll be well-positioned to seize new opportunities and maintain a thriving freelance career.

USE CASE: MONETIZING AI AUTOMATION AND CONTENT CREATION

In today's fast-paced digital world, turning ideas into income often feels like an uphill battle—until AI enters the picture. This is the story of Sophia, an aspiring entrepreneur who used AI to automate content creation, streamline her workflow, and transform her passion into a profitable online brand—with minimal effort and maximum impact.

Sophia had always dreamed of starting her own business, but the idea of managing everything herself felt overwhelming. She loved creating content and sharing ideas, but the thought of constantly brainstorming, designing, writing, and posting seemed like a never-ending grind. That was until she discovered the power of AI. With the right tools and a clear strategy, Sophia realized she could automate much of the process and build a thriving social media brand with minimal manual effort.

One evening, sitting at her desk with a cup of tea in hand, Sophia decided to take the plunge. She began by choosing her niche. After some research assisted by Perplexity, she settled on sustainable living—a topic close to her heart and gaining traction online. She envisioned a brand that shared tips on eco-friendly practices, product recommendations, and how-to guides for living a greener life. With her niche defined, she outlined her goals: grow an engaged audience on Instagram and YouTube, monetize through affiliate marketing and digital products, and eventually become a thought leader in the space.

The next step was setting up her toolkit. Sophia had heard about AI tools that could streamline content creation and publishing, so she dove into research. She signed up for **OwlyWriter AI**, which promised to generate social media captions and post ideas tailored to her brand's voice. For longer content like blog posts or video scripts, Sophia opted for **GPT-4o**, an advanced language model capable of producing high-quality drafts. To create visuals, she chose **Canva**, which offered AI-powered design suggestions to make professional-looking graphics quickly. Finally, to tie everything together, she set up **Make.com**, an automation platform that could connect all her tools and create seamless workflows.

With her tools ready, Sophia began generating content ideas. She opened OwlyWriter AI and typed in "sustainable living tips." Within seconds, the tool provided a list of engaging post ideas: "10 Easy Swaps for a Zero-Waste Kitchen," "How to Build an Eco-Friendly Morning Routine," and "The Best Reusable Products for Everyday Life." Excited by the suggestions, she saved them to her content calendar.

Next came content creation. Using GPT-4o, Sophia drafted a blog post titled "5 Simple Ways to Reduce Plastic Waste." The AI-generated text was well-written and informative but needed some tweaking to match her tone. She edited the draft, adding personal anecdotes about her journey toward sustainability. For Instagram captions, OwlyWriter AI crafted concise yet compelling copy that paired perfectly with her visuals.

For graphics, Sophia turned to Canva. She uploaded photos of reusable products she used at home and let Canva's AI suggest layouts and fonts that matched her brand aesthetic. Within minutes, she had polished designs ready for posting. For video content on YouTube, Sophia experimented with **Pictory.ai**, which transformed her blog posts into short videos by pairing text with stock footage and captions.

Despite the efficiency of these tools, Sophia knew the importance of maintaining authenticity. Every piece of content went through her final review. She used **Grammarly** to check for errors and ensure consistency in tone before publishing anything. Adding personal touches—like sharing her favorite eco-friendly recipes or photos from her zero-waste lifestyle—helped build trust with her audience.

Once the content was ready, it was time to schedule and publish. Sophia used **Hootsuite** to plan posts across Instagram and YouTube weeks in advance. OwlyWriter's integration with Hootsuite allowed her to fill up her calendar quickly by pulling directly from the drafts she'd created earlier. To make things even easier, she set up automated workflows in Make.com. Whenever she finished editing a blog post in WordPress, it automatically generated social media captions using GPT-4o and scheduled them in Hootsuite.

As days turned into weeks, Sophia began seeing results. Her Instagram following grew steadily as people engaged with her tips and shared her posts with friends. On YouTube, viewers appreciated the clarity of her videos and left comments asking for more advice on sustainable living.

Sophia monitored performance metrics regularly to keep improving. She used Instagram's built-in analytics to track engagement rates and Google Analytics to measure traffic on her blog. When she noticed that posts about eco-friendly product recommendations performed exceptionally well, she adjusted her strategy to include more of that content.

With an engaged audience now in place, Sophia moved on to monetization. She signed up for affiliate programs with brands that aligned with her values—companies selling reusable water bottles or compostable packaging—and started earning commissions every time someone purchased through her links. She also created a digital product: an eBook titled "The Beginner's Guide to Sustainable Living," which she wrote with help from GPT-4o. The eBook became an instant hit among her followers.

As time went on, Sophia scaled her operations further. She hired a virtual assistant to handle customer inquiries about her eBook and invested in advanced AI tools like **Sprinklr** for social listening, which allowed her to stay ahead of trends in sustainability conversations online. She even launched a podcast where she interviewed experts in the field, diversifying her content formats while continuing to automate much of the production process.

One day, as Sophia reviewed her automated workflows over tea—the same way this journey had started—she marveled at how far she'd come. Her daily routine no longer involved scrambling for content ideas or manually posting updates across platforms; instead, it revolved around engaging with her audience and brainstorming new ways to grow.

Sophia's favorite workflow was still one of the first automations she'd set up: industry news articles were fed into Make.com each morning as inspiration for new posts. These articles were sent directly to GPT-4o for caption generation before being polished by OwlyWriter AI and paired with visuals from Canva—all without requiring any manual input from Sophia herself.

Building a social media brand had once seemed daunting—but by leveraging AI tools effectively, Sophia had turned what could have been an exhausting grind into an efficient system that allowed creativity and strategy to take center stage.

Her story is proof that anyone can succeed as a content creator when they combine passion with innovative automation strategies—and that even in a world dominated by technology, authenticity remains key to building meaningful connections online.

7
THE FUTURE OF AI

Imagine waking up to a home that seems to anticipate your every need. The curtains gently open as the sun rises, your coffee brews just how you like it, and the thermostat adjusts to your perfect temperature—all without lifting a finger. This isn't a glimpse into a distant future; it's the power of AI and the Internet of Things (IoT) working harmoniously to create a seamlessly connected ecosystem. This chapter is your gateway into understanding how AI and IoT technologies are transforming the way we live, work, and interact with the world around us. It's not just about smart homes; it's about smart living.

The synergy between AI and IoT is reshaping industries, starting with smart home automation. Picture your home equipped with IoT devices like smart lights, thermostats, and security cameras, all interconnected and controlled by AI. These AI-integrated IoT devices learn your routines and preferences, providing a personalized experience that enhances comfort and efficiency. Imagine never having to worry about leaving the lights on or adjusting the thermostat; your home takes care of these tasks for you. However, the impact of AI-IoT integration extends beyond the home, influencing industrial settings through enhanced predictive maintenance. In manufacturing facilities, IoT sensors collect real-time data on equipment performance, while AI analyzes this data to predict when maintenance is needed. This proactive approach reduces downtime, minimizes costs, and prolongs the life of machinery, optimizing industrial processes.

The benefits of AI-IoT integration are vast and varied, with applications reaching into sectors like healthcare and urban management. In healthcare, IoT devices monitor patient vitals remotely, while AI analyzes the data to provide insights and support telemedicine services. Imagine a world where healthcare professionals can monitor patients in real-time, making informed decisions without the need for constant hospital visits. This integration improves patient outcomes and reduces healthcare costs by enabling early intervention. In smart cities, AI and IoT work together to optimize traffic flow, manage energy consumption, and enhance public safety. Picture a city where traffic lights adapt to real-time conditions, reducing congestion and emissions, or where streetlights dim when no pedestrians are present, conserving energy. These smart city solutions improve urban living and contribute to sustainability efforts.

However, the integration of AI and IoT comes with its own set of challenges. One primary concern is ensuring data privacy and security in interconnected systems. With vast amounts of data being collected and transmitted between devices, the risk of data breaches and unauthorized access is significant. Implementing robust security measures, like encryption and secure authentication, is crucial to protect sensitive information. Interoperability issues between diverse IoT devices also pose a challenge. Different devices may use varying protocols and standards, making seamless communication difficult. To overcome this, industry stakeholders must collaborate to develop universal standards and protocols that ensure compatibility and integration across devices.

Looking to the future, the potential of AI-IoT technologies is immense, with the promise of transforming industries and addressing global challenges. AI-driven environmental monitoring systems could track air quality, water levels, and wildlife populations, providing valuable data to support conservation efforts. Imagine using AI and IoT to monitor the health of ecosystems in real-time, enabling swift action to mitigate environmental threats. In agriculture, AI-IoT integration might optimize water usage, track crop health, and manage resources more efficiently, contributing to sustainable farming practices. As these technologies continue to evolve, they hold the potential to create a more connected, efficient, and sustainable world.

Interactive Element: Reflection

Take a moment to consider how AI and IoT are already a part of your life. Do you have a smart device at home, like a thermostat or speaker? How does it change your daily routine? Imagine how these technologies might evolve in the next five years. What aspects of your life could they improve?

AGENTIC AI: THE NEXT EVOLUTION OF AI

While generative AI models like ChatGPT have been revolutionary in generating human-like text, their capabilities are limited to producing content based on the input they receive. In contrast, agentic AI represents a paradigm shift, enabling AI systems to perform tasks autonomously, make independent decisions, and adapt to new information without continuous human intervention.

There are several key areas where agentic AI is poised to surpass traditional generative models. Agentic AI systems are designed to understand objectives and execute tasks without explicit step-by-step instructions. This autonomy allows them to handle complex operations, such as managing supply chains or personalizing customer interactions, by making real-time decisions based on dynamic data inputs.

Unlike ChatGPT, which primarily functions as a standalone conversational agent, agentic AI can seamlessly integrate with various software and platforms. This integration enables it to access and process information across different domains, facilitating more comprehensive solutions and streamlined workflows.

Agentic AI systems possess the capability to learn from their experiences and adapt their behavior over time. This continuous learning process allows them to improve performance, anticipate future trends, and proactively address potential challenges, enhancing efficiency and effectiveness in various applications.

Potential challenges associated with the deployment of agentic AI include ethical considerations, data privacy concerns, and the need for robust governance frameworks to ensure responsible usage. As these systems become more integrated into critical decision-making processes, it is imperative to establish clear guidelines and oversight mechanisms to mitigate risks and ensure alignment with human values.

The takeaway here is that while ChatGPT has laid the groundwork for AI-human interactions, the future lies in the development and implementation of agentic AI systems. These advanced models are expected to revolutionize various industries by performing tasks with a level of autonomy and sophistication that far exceeds the capabilities of current generative AI, effectively making tools like ChatGPT appear rudimentary in comparison.

INNOVATIONS IN AI: KEEPING PACE WITH CHANGE

Imagine a world where computers process information at speeds once thought impossible. This vision is becoming a reality with quantum computing. In traditional computing, bits are the smallest unit and exist in a state of either 0 or 1. Quantum computing, however, uses quantum bits, or qubits, which can simultaneously represent and store data in multiple states. This allows quantum computers to perform complex calculations at unprecedented speeds, revolutionizing industries that rely on data-intensive processes. For instance, in pharmaceuticals, quantum computing can accelerate drug discovery by simulating molecular interactions in ways that traditional computers cannot. The potential here is vast, offering solutions to problems previously deemed unsolvable.

Another exciting advancement is neuromorphic computing, which mimics the human brain's architecture to create more efficient AI algorithms. Unlike traditional AI models that require vast amounts of data and energy, neuromorphic systems are designed to be energy-efficient and capable of real-time learning. These systems excel in tasks like pattern recognition and sensory processing, making them ideal for applications in robotics and autonomous vehicles. Imagine a robot that can navigate a complex environment with the same ease as a human, processing sensory input in real-time to make decisions. Neuromorphic computing is paving the way for AI that learns faster and adapts more efficiently to new situations.

In the realm of transportation, AI is making significant strides in autonomous vehicle technology. Picture a car that drives itself, navigating busy streets with precision and safety. AI enhances navigation systems by processing data from sensors and cameras, allowing vehicles to detect obstacles, interpret road signs, and make split-second decisions. This technology promises to reduce accidents and traffic congestion, making roads safer for everyone. Beyond Earth, AI is also revolutionizing space exploration. AI-powered robotic systems are being used to collect and analyze data from distant planets, helping scientists understand the universe's mysteries. With AI, space missions can operate autonomously, even in the most remote and hostile environments, pushing the boundaries of what we can explore and discover.

AI's influence extends to the creative industries, reshaping how art and music are produced. AI-generated art challenges traditional notions of creativity by using algorithms to create unique and compelling pieces. Artists are collaborating with AI to explore new artistic expressions, pushing the limits of their creativity. In music, AI composes original scores and even collaborates with musicians to produce innovative sounds. This fusion of technology and creativity opens up new possibilities for artistic expression, allowing for the creation of works that were previously unimaginable. In film and media production, AI enhances visual effects and creates realistic simulations that captivate audiences. AI can analyze scripts, suggest plot developments, and even generate realistic character animations, transforming the storytelling process.

While the potential of AI is enormous, its rapid advancement brings challenges that must be addressed. Ethical considerations are paramount in AI development. Ensuring that AI systems are fair, transparent, and accountable is crucial to prevent bias and discrimination. Developers must prioritize the ethical implications of AI, ensuring that these technologies benefit society as a whole. Additionally, balancing innovation with regulation and oversight is essential to foster responsible AI development. Policymakers and industry leaders must collaborate to create frameworks supporting innovation while protecting individual rights and privacy. As AI continues to evolve, it is vital to address these challenges head-on, ensuring that this transformative technology serves as a force for good.

AI IN HEALTHCARE: TRANSFORMING PATIENT CARE

Imagine visiting a doctor and getting a diagnosis not after lengthy tests but almost instantly, thanks to a quick scan analyzed by AI.

This isn't just the stuff of science fiction; it's the reality of AI-driven diagnostics. AI has revolutionized how we detect diseases, using advanced imaging analysis to catch them early. Think of AI as a highly trained eye that can spot abnormalities in medical scans faster and sometimes more accurately than a human can. It processes thousands of images, identifying patterns and markers that might indicate a problem, such as tumors or fractures, helping doctors make informed decisions quickly. This ability to detect issues early can lead to more effective treatment plans and ultimately save lives.

Beyond diagnostics, AI is making waves in patient management. Imagine being able to monitor your health from home, with data sent directly to your healthcare provider. AI enables remote monitoring through wearable devices that track vital signs and other health metrics. Healthcare providers can be alerted immediately if anything unusual is detected, allowing for timely intervention. This isn't just convenient; it transforms how patient care is delivered, particularly for those with chronic conditions who require continuous monitoring. Moreover, AI-powered virtual health assistants are becoming essential in educating patients about their conditions, treatment options, and medications. These assistants offer reliable information, helping patients manage their health and make informed choices about their care.

In the realm of drug discovery, AI is a game-changer. Developing new drugs is traditionally a lengthy and costly process, but AI speeds things up significantly. It analyzes vast amounts of data to identify potential drug candidates, highlighting those most likely to succeed in clinical trials. AI simulations can also predict how these drugs will interact with the human body, reducing the need for extensive trial and error. This cuts down on the time it takes to bring new treatments to market and lowers costs, making healthcare innovations more accessible. The efficiency AI brings to drug discovery holds the promise of accelerating the development of treatments for diseases that currently lack effective options.

Yet, with these advancements come ethical considerations that cannot be overlooked. In healthcare, patient privacy is paramount. AI systems rely on large datasets, often containing sensitive information, to function effectively. It's crucial to balance the benefits of data-driven innovation with the need to protect individual privacy. Clear guidelines and robust security measures must be in place to ensure data is used responsibly and remains confidential. Furthermore, as AI becomes more integrated into healthcare, we must ensure equitable access to these technologies. It's vital that all patients, regardless of geography or socioeconomic status, benefit from AI-enhanced healthcare. Otherwise, we risk widening the gap between those with access to advanced medical care and those without access.

Case Study: AI in Action

Consider a hospital that has integrated AI into its diagnostic processes. In this setting, AI analyzes MRI scans to detect early signs of diseases like Alzheimer's. This early detection allows for intervention before symptoms become severe, potentially slowing the disease's progression. The hospital also uses AI to personalize treatment plans, analyzing patient data to recommend therapies that are most likely to be effective. This personalized approach improves patient outcomes and optimizes resource use, ensuring treatments are tailored to individual needs. By embracing AI, the hospital enhances its diagnostic capabilities and patient care, illustrating AI's transformative potential in healthcare.

As AI continues to evolve, its role in healthcare will only expand, offering new ways to improve patient care and outcomes.

AI AND ETHICAL AI DEVELOPMENT: A BALANCED APPROACH

Imagine AI as a powerful tool that can change lives, improve industries, and push the boundaries of what's possible. But, like any tool, its impact depends on how we use it. When it comes to developing AI, ethics play a crucial role in guiding responsible creation. Fairness and transparency are foundational ethical principles that ensure AI algorithms act without bias and are understandable to those they impact. Think about it this way: if an AI system predicts whether someone qualifies for a loan, it should do so based on accurate data, without discrimination, and with clear reasoning. Transparency allows users to see how decisions are made, which fosters trust. Alongside this, accountability and human oversight ensure that AI systems remain tools for humans, with people ready to intervene if things go awry.

Yet, implementing these ethical principles isn't without its challenges. One of the most significant hurdles is mitigating bias in AI models and data sets. It's not uncommon for these systems to learn from flawed data, perpetuating existing biases and inequalities. For example, suppose an AI model is trained on data that lacks diversity. In that case, it may make skewed predictions that unfairly disadvantage certain groups. Addressing the societal impacts of AI automation also poses ethical dilemmas. Automation can boost efficiency but may lead to job losses, affecting livelihoods and communities. Balancing these benefits and drawbacks requires careful consideration and planning, ensuring that AI advancements uplift rather than undermine society.

To navigate these challenges, practical strategies for ethical AI development are essential. Establishing ethical guidelines and oversight committees can help organizations maintain focus on ethical practices. These committees review AI projects, ensuring they align with ethical standards and address potential risks. Engaging diverse stakeholders in AI development processes is also critical. By involving people from varied backgrounds, developers can gain insights into different perspectives, which enhances the system's fairness and relevance. This collaborative approach helps identify potential biases and encourages inclusivity, making AI systems more effective and equitable.

Real-world examples of organizations successfully implementing ethical AI practices are inspiring. Some companies are prioritizing diversity and inclusion within their AI teams, recognizing that diverse viewpoints lead to better outcomes. Others are launching initiatives that use AI to tackle social and environmental issues. Consider a company leveraging AI to monitor air quality and alert communities about pollution levels, empowering people to make informed decisions about their health. These examples demonstrate that when organizations are committed to ethical AI, they can create technologies that benefit society in meaningful and impactful ways.

PREPARING FOR AI DISRUPTION: ADAPTING TO CHANGE

Imagine waking up one day to find that the skills you learned in school are no longer enough. That's the reality we're stepping into as AI continues to evolve. The workforce is transforming, and with it, the nature of jobs. Industries that once relied heavily on human labor are now integrating AI, which can perform repetitive and data-heavy tasks with remarkable speed and accuracy. This shift means that many roles might change or disappear, but new opportunities are emerging. As AI handles tasks like data entry, customer service, and even some medical diagnostics, it frees up human workers to focus on more complex and creative work. This can lead to job displacement but also paves the way for new jobs requiring skills in AI management and development.

It's not just the workforce that's changing; consumer behavior is also evolving. People are becoming accustomed to personalized experiences, thanks to AI-driven recommendations and customer service. This demand for customization and efficiency is pushing businesses to innovate, leading to a shift in market dynamics. Companies that fail to adapt risk falling behind. To stay competitive, businesses must embrace AI-driven strategies, using data to understand customer needs and tailor their products and services accordingly. Those who leverage AI can gain a significant advantage, attracting more customers and increasing loyalty by offering unique and personalized experiences.

Adaptation is key for individuals and organizations looking to thrive in this new landscape. One effective strategy is reskilling and upskilling the workforce. This involves training employees in new skills relevant to an AI-driven world, such as data analysis, machine learning, and AI ethics. Individuals can remain valuable in the job market by investing in education and training. At the same time, organizations can build a workforce ready to tackle future challenges. Embracing AI-driven innovation in business strategies is also crucial. Companies should explore how AI can streamline operations, enhance decision-making, and improve customer engagement. By integrating AI into their business models, they can stay ahead of the curve and drive growth.

Policy and regulation have crucial roles to play in managing AI disruption. Governments and regulatory bodies must develop frameworks supporting workforce transitions, ensuring that people displaced by AI have access to training and job opportunities. Policies that encourage responsible AI innovation are also essential. These should focus on promoting transparency, accountability, and fairness in AI systems while protecting individual rights and privacy. By creating a supportive regulatory environment, policymakers can help mitigate the negative impacts of AI disruption and foster a more inclusive and equitable economy.

The societal impact of AI is profound and multifaceted. Ensuring social equity and inclusion in AI-driven economies is essential so everyone benefits from technological advancements. This means addressing disparities in access to AI education and opportunities, particularly for underrepresented groups. Fostering public awareness and understanding of AI technologies is also vital. By educating people about AI's benefits and risks, we can build trust and encourage responsible use. Public awareness campaigns, workshops, and community engagement can help demystify AI, empowering individuals to make informed decisions in an increasingly AI-driven world.

LIFELONG LEARNING IN AI: STAYING AHEAD OF THE CURVE

In a world where AI is constantly advancing, staying updated isn't a luxury—it's a necessity. The rapid pace of technological change means that what you know today might be outdated tomorrow. This is where the concept of lifelong learning comes into play. It's about continuously acquiring knowledge and skills to keep up with these evolving technologies. Adapting to these changes ensures you remain competitive in the job market. Think of it as an ongoing process, a bit like tending to a garden. You need to nurture your skills, pulling out the weeds of outdated information and planting seeds of new knowledge. This approach prepares you for shifts in the AI landscape and keeps you relevant and valuable in your career.

Fortunately, there are plenty of resources and opportunities available. Online courses and certifications are an excellent way to learn about AI and machine learning. Platforms like Coursera and edX offer courses from top universities, allowing you to learn at your own pace. These courses cover everything from the basics to advanced topics, providing a comprehensive education. Certifications, on the other hand, can boost your resume, signaling to employers that you're serious about your skills. Beyond online learning, consider attending workshops, conferences, and networking events. These gatherings are not just about learning; they're about connecting with others in the AI community. They offer a chance to hear from experts, exchange ideas, and even collaborate on projects. It's a dynamic way to stay engaged and informed.

Collaboration and knowledge sharing play crucial roles in learning about AI. By participating in research and development projects, you can gain hands-on experience and insights from others. Engaging with AI communities and professional networks helps you learn from peers, share your experiences, and gain new perspectives. It's akin to joining a club where everyone shares the same passion. These interactions often lead to new ideas and collaborations, enriching your understanding and sparking innovation. They create a support system, offering encouragement and guidance as you navigate the complexities of AI.

Cross-disciplinary learning adds another layer to your education. Integrating AI knowledge with other fields opens up new possibilities for innovation. Consider how AI can enhance interdisciplinary research, such as using AI algorithms in biology to analyze genetic data. Or how combining AI skills with domain-specific expertise can lead to breakthroughs in fields like finance, where AI models can predict market trends with precision. This blending of knowledge not only broadens your skill set but also makes you more adaptable and creative. It empowers you to think outside the box, applying AI in novel ways to solve complex problems.

As we wrap up our exploration of lifelong learning in AI, remember that the journey doesn't end here. In the next chapter, we'll delve into AI's applications in real-world scenarios, uncovering how these technologies are shaping industries and redefining the way we live and work.

8

RESOURCES TO TAKE ON YOUR AI JOURNEY

Think of this chapter as your personal AI survival kit. You've come a long way already, absorbing all sorts of info about the world of artificial intelligence. You're probably feeling a mix of excitement, maybe a little bit of overwhelm, and definitely a burning curiosity to learn more. And that's exactly where you should be!

The thing about AI is that it's not a destination; it's a *journey*. It's constantly evolving, with new tools, techniques, and breakthroughs popping up faster than you can say "neural network." That's why it's super important to arm yourself with the right resources to stay ahead of the curve and keep your AI skills sharp.

Let's be real, the internet is overflowing with information about AI. But not all of it is created equal. You've got your fair share of clickbait articles, confusing jargon, and outdated tutorials. Sifting through all that noise to find the *good* stuff can feel like searching for a needle in a haystack.

I've curated a list of resources that I personally find valuable and trustworthy. These aren't just random links I found on Google; these are the websites, books, communities, and tools that I rely on to stay informed, inspired, and connected in the AI world.

Think of these resources as your trusty companions on your AI quest. Whether you're looking to dive deeper into a specific topic, connect with fellow AI enthusiasts, or find the perfect tool to build your next AI masterpiece, this chapter has got you covered.

We'll be covering a range of resources, from online courses and tutorials to research papers and industry blogs. We'll also explore some of the best communities and forums where you can connect with other AI learners and experts. And, of course, we'll take a look at some of the most useful tools and libraries that can help you build and deploy your own AI applications.

So, grab your favorite beverage, settle in, and get ready to load up your AI toolkit. I want to empower you to continue your AI journey with confidence. Let's dive in and discover the resources that will help you stay curious, keep learning, and build amazing things with AI!

CONTINUING EDUCATION: ESSENTIAL AI RESOURCES

Online Learning Platforms

First stop on our resource journey: online learning platforms. These are your go-to spots for structured learning experiences.

1. **Coursera**: Home to the famous Andrew Ng's Machine Learning course. They've got a ton of AI and ML courses from top universities.
2. **edX**: Another heavyweight in the MOOC world. Check out their MicroMasters programs in AI if you're looking for something more comprehensive.
3. **Fast.ai**: If you're into practical, hands-on learning, Fast.ai is

your jam. Their "Practical Deep Learning for Coders" course is legendary.

4. **Udacity**: Their AI Nanodegree programs are pretty solid if you're looking for a more intensive, project-based learning experience.
5. **DataCamp**: Great for data science fundamentals, which are crucial for AI.

YouTube Channels

Sometimes you just want to kick back and learn through video. Here are some YouTube channels that'll keep you informed and entertained:

1. **Two Minute Papers:** Quick, engaging summaries of cutting-edge AI research.
2. **Lex Fridman**: In-depth interviews with AI researchers and thought leaders.
3. **3Blue1Brown**: Beautiful animations explaining math concepts crucial for AI.
4. **Sentdex**: Practical tutorials on building AI projects.
5. **AI Coffee Break with Letitia**: Bite-sized explanations of AI concepts.

Blogs and Websites

For those times when you want to dive deep into written content:

1. **Towards Data Science** on Medium: A goldmine of articles on AI, ML, and data science.
2. **ArXiv**: The go-to place for the latest research papers in AI and ML.
3. **Distill.pub**: Beautiful, interactive explanations of complex AI concepts.

4. **OpenAI Blog**: Stay updated on the latest from one of the leading AI research companies.
5. **Google AI Blog**: Another great source for cutting-edge AI developments.

Books

Sometimes, you just can't beat a good book. Here are some must-reads:

1. **"Deep Learning" by Ian Goodfellow, Yoshua Bengio, and Aaron Courville**: The deep learning bible.
2. **"Artificial Intelligence: A Modern Approach" by Stuart Russell and Peter Norvig**: A comprehensive overview of AI.
3. **"Hands-On Machine Learning with Scikit-Learn, Keras, and TensorFlow" by Aurélien Géron**: Great for practical implementation.
4. **"The Hundred-Page Machine Learning Book" by Andriy Burkov**: A concise yet comprehensive guide to ML.
5. **"AI Superpowers" by Kai-Fu Lee**: For a broader perspective on AI's impact on society.

Podcasts

For learning on the go:

1. **AI Podcast** by Lex Fridman: In-depth conversations with AI researchers and industry leaders.
2. **Data Skeptic**: Breaks down AI and data science concepts in an accessible way.
3. **Practical AI**: Focuses on real-world applications of AI.
4. **The TWIML AI Podcast**: Covers the latest in machine learning and AI.
5. **AI in Business**: Great for understanding AI's impact on various industries.

Tools and Libraries

Now, let's talk about the tools that'll help you actually build AI systems:

1. **TensorFlow**: Google's open-source ML library. Great for building and deploying ML models.
2. **PyTorch**: Facebook's ML library. Known for its flexibility and ease of use in research.
3. **Scikit-learn**: A user-friendly library for classical ML algorithms.
4. **Keras**: A high-level neural network library that runs on top of TensorFlow.
5. **OpenAI Gym**: For reinforcement learning enthusiasts.
6. **Jupyter Notebooks**: The go-to tool for interactive computing and data visualization.
7. **Google Colab**: Free cloud-based Jupyter notebooks with GPU access.

Communities and Forums

Because sometimes you need to connect with fellow AI enthusiasts:

1. **Reddit**: Check out r/MachineLearning, r/artificial, and r/learnmachinelearning.
2. **Stack Overflow**: For when you're stuck on a coding problem.
3. **Kaggle**: Great for competitions, datasets, and connecting with other data scientists.
4. **AI Stack Exchange**: A Q&A site specifically for AI and ML questions.
5. **GitHub**: Follow AI projects, contribute to open-source, and showcase your own work.

Conferences and Events

To stay updated on the latest in AI and network with others in the field:

1. **NeurIPS (Neural Information Processing Systems)**: One of the biggest AI conferences.
2. **ICML (International Conference on Machine Learning)**: Another major conference in the field.
3. **ICLR (International Conference on Learning Representations)**: Focuses on representation learning.
4. **AI for Good Global Summit**: Explores how AI can address global challenges.
5. **Local Meetups**: Check Meetup.com for AI and ML gatherings in your area.

Newsletters

To get curated AI content delivered straight to your inbox:

1. **Import AI**: Jack Clark's weekly newsletter on AI progress.
2. **The Algorithm** by MIT Technology Review: Covers the latest in AI and its impact.
3. **AI Weekly**: A curated list of the most interesting AI news and resources.
4. **The Batch** by Andrew Ng: Weekly AI news and learning resources.
5. **Data Elixir**: A weekly newsletter covering data science and AI.

Research Papers and Journals

For those who want to dive into the cutting edge of AI research:

1. **arXiv.org**: The go-to preprint server for AI and ML papers.

2. **Journal of Machine Learning Research (JMLR)**: A leading open-access journal in the field.
3. **IEEE Transactions on Pattern Analysis and Machine Intelligence**: Covers a wide range of AI topics.
4. **Nature Machine Intelligence**: High-impact AI research from the Nature publishing group.
5. **Papers With Code**: Provides code implementations alongside research papers.

Datasets and Benchmarks

Because every AI project needs data:

1. **UCI Machine Learning Repository**: A large collection of datasets for ML.
2. **Kaggle Datasets**: A platform for finding and publishing datasets.
3. **Google Dataset Search**: A search engine for datasets.
4. **ImageNet**: A large visual database designed for visual object recognition research.
5. **MNIST**: The "Hello World" of ML datasets, great for beginners.

Ethics and Responsible AI Resources

As AI becomes more prevalent, understanding its ethical implications is crucial:

1. **AI Ethics Guidelines Global Inventory** by Algorithm Watch: A collection of AI ethics guidelines from around the world.
2. **Ethics of AI and Robotics** on Stanford Encyclopedia of Philosophy: A comprehensive overview of AI ethics.
3. **AI Now Institute**: Research on the social implications of AI.

4. **The Institute for Ethical AI & Machine Learning**: Practical frameworks for responsible AI development.
5. **Fairness, Accountability, and Transparency in Machine Learning (FAT/ML)**: A community of researchers and practitioners.

Career Resources

For those looking to turn their AI passion into a career:

1. **AI Jobs**: A job board specifically for AI-related positions.
2. **Machine Learning Mastery**: Offers practical advice on building a career in ML.
3. **Crunchbase**: Great for researching AI startups and companies.
4. **LinkedIn**: Follow AI thought leaders and join AI-related groups.
5. **AngelList**: Another great resource for finding jobs at AI startups.

Keeping Up with AI News

To stay on top of the rapidly evolving AI landscape:

1. **AI News**: A dedicated AI news site.
2. **MIT Technology Review**: Often features in-depth AI articles.
3. **VentureBeat AI**: Covers AI from a business and application perspective.
4. **The Verge**: Often features accessible articles on AI developments.
5. **Wired**: Provides thoughtful coverage on AI and its societal impact.

AI TOOLS: THE BEST OF THE BEST TO GET STUFF DONE

Generative AI (Text, Image, Video)

1. **ChatGPT (OpenAI)** – Text generation, reasoning, coding
2. **MidJourney** – AI art & image generation
3. **DALL-E 3 (OpenAI)** – Image generation via text prompts
4. **Runway Gen-2** – Text-to-video & video editing
5. **Stable Diffusion** – Open-source image generation

AI Chatbots & Virtual Assistants

6. **ChatGPT (w/ GPTs)** – Custom AI assistants
7. **Claude (Anthropic)** – Conversational AI, analysis
8. **Jasper Chat** – AI writer + chatbot for business
9. **Poe (Quora)** – Multi-AI model chat platform
10. **Perplexity AI** – AI search + chatbot

AI Coding & Development Tools

11. **GitHub Copilot** – Code completion & suggestion
12. **Replit AI** – AI coding in browser IDE
13. **Cursor (AI IDE)** – AI-assisted code editor
14. **Amazon CodeWhisperer** – AI coding assistant (AWS focused)
15. **Tabnine** – Code autocompletion AI

AI Video & Audio Editing/Creation

16. **Synthesia** – AI video avatars & narrators
17. **Pictory** – AI video creation from text
18. **Descript** – Video & audio editing w/ AI
19. **ElevenLabs** – AI voice generation & cloning

20. **Runway Gen-2** – AI video generation (text-to-video)

AI for Business Automation (Productivity, CRM, Sales)

21. **Zapier AI** – Workflow automation with AI
22. **Notion AI** – AI for productivity & docs
23. **ChatGPT Enterprise** – AI for business & internal tools
24. **Copy.ai (Workflows)** – AI workflow automation
25. **HubSpot AI** – CRM & sales AI tools

AI Marketing & Copywriting

26. **Jasper.ai** – AI marketing copy & campaigns
27. **Copy.ai** – Marketing, email, product copy
28. **Writesonic** – AI content creation platform
29. **Anyword** – AI copy for ads & conversion
30. **NeuralText** – SEO-optimized AI writing

AI Data Analytics & Visualization

31. **ChatGPT + Code Interpreter (ADA)** – Data analysis, Python scripting
32. **Tableau (AI features)** – AI-powered data visualization
33. **Power BI (Copilot)** – Microsoft's AI for data analytics
34. **Polymer Search** – No-code AI data visualization
35. **MonkeyLearn** – AI text analytics

AI for Design (Graphics, UX/UI, Web Design)

36. **Canva AI (Magic Design, Magic Write)** – AI for graphic & web design
37. **Uizard** – AI web & app design
38. **Designs.ai** – AI-generated logos & graphics
39. **Galileo AI** – AI UI/UX design from text prompts

40. **Khroma** – AI color palette generator

AI for Customer Support (Helpdesk, Ticketing, Bots)

41. **Forethought AI** – AI helpdesk & ticketing
42. **Ada** – AI customer service bots
43. **Ultimate.ai** – AI customer support automation
44. **Intercom AI** – AI chatbots & support automation
45. **Tidio AI** – AI chatbot for sales & support

AI for Research & Summarization (Knowledge Work, Legal, Academic)

46. **Perplexity AI** – AI search & research summarizer
47. **Consensus** – AI academic paper summarizer
48. **Scite.ai** – AI for academic research insights
49. **Elicit.org** – AI research assistant (literature)
50. **Genei** – AI summarizer for research papers

AI for Building Apps

51. **Builder.ai** – AI-generated mobile & web apps from plain descriptions
52. **Bubble (with AI Plugins)** – No-code platform with AI-assisted workflows & logic
53. **Glide AI** – AI-generated mobile & web apps from spreadsheets
54. **Uizard** – AI-generated app UI/UX prototypes from text prompts
55. **Debuild** – AI-generated React web apps & UI from text prompts

These categories and tools dominate AI-driven workflows right now, but the winners can change fast—especially as open-source and niche-specific AI solutions keep evolving. If you're looking to leverage these in business, automation, or content creation, knowing which ones integrate well with your existing stack is key.

Phew! That's a lot of resources, right? But here's the thing: you don't need to dive into all of these at once. Think of this chapter as your AI buffet – sample a bit of everything, then go back for seconds on the stuff you really enjoy. Remember, the key to staying on top of AI isn't about consuming every single piece of content out there. It's about finding the resources that resonate with you, that keep you curious and excited about learning. So, start exploring. Maybe pick one or two resources from each category that catch your eye. Bookmark this chapter and come back to it whenever you're looking for something new to dive into. And most importantly, don't forget to apply what you learn. Build projects, participate in discussions, share your knowledge with others. That's how you'll truly grow on your AI journey. Keep learning, stay curious, and have fun exploring the fascinating world of AI!

But wait, there is more.

100 CHATGPT PROMPTS (OR ANY OF YOUR FAVORITE GENERATIVE AI PLATFORMS)

ChatGPT is like a digital genie in a bottle, waiting for your command. To help you make the most of it, I've compiled a treasure trove of 100 creative prompts. Whether you're planning meals or organizing your day, these prompts can transform chaos into order.

Email & Communication

- **Email Drafting** – Draft an email to [Recipient's name] regarding [Specific Topic or Request]
- **Writing Meeting Minutes** – Write meeting minutes based on the following conversation: [Insert Conversation Here]

- **Writing a Letter of Recommendation** – Draft a letter of recommendation for [Insert Person's Name and Achievements Here]
- **Feedback Request** – Help me draft a feedback request email to my team for this project: [Insert Project Details Here]

Content Creation & Writing

- **Brainstorming Ideas** – Generate ten creative ideas for [Specific Project or Problem]
- **Content Proofreading** – Proofread this text for grammatical errors and readability: [Insert Text Here]
- **Content Summarization** – Summarize this article or document. The summary should be concise and easy to understand: [Insert Link or Text Here]
- **Writing Press Release** – Draft a press release for this new product launch: [Insert Product Details Here]
- **Writing a Speech** – Write a 5-minute speech on the topic of [Insert Topic Here]
- **Writing Marketing Copy** – Write compelling marketing copy for [Insert Product or Service Here]
- **Report Writing** – Write a report on the following data: [Insert Data Here]

Coding & Tech Support

- **Coding Help** – Help me understand this piece of code: [Insert Code Here]
- **Design Feedback** – Provide constructive feedback on this design description: [Insert Description Here]

Education & Research

- **Book Suggestions** – Suggest five books on the topic of [Insert Topic Here]
- **Research Topic Suggestions** – Suggest five research topics in the field of [Insert Field or Interest Here]
- **Learning Path Suggestions** – Suggest a learning path for mastering [Insert Skill Here]
- **Ted Talk Summary** – Summarize the key points of this Ted Talk: [Insert Link Here]
- **Trivia Questions Creation** – Create ten trivia questions about [Insert Topic Here]

Personal Development & Well-Being

- **Self-reflection Questions** – Provide me with five thought-provoking self-reflection questions
- **Daily Journal Prompt Suggestions** – Provide five journaling prompts for self-improvement
- **Daily Affirmations** – Provide me with five positive daily affirmations
- **Meditation Instructions** – Guide me through a 10-minute meditation session focusing on mindfulness
- **Role-Playing Scenarios** – Create a role-playing scenario for [Insert Desired Skill or Situation Here]

Language & Translation

- **Speech Translation** – Translate this English text into [Insert Desired Language Here]: [Insert English Text Here]

Travel & Tourism

- **Travel Itinerary Planning** – Create a 7-day travel itinerary for a trip to [Destination], including top attractions, local food recommendations, and hidden gems.
- **Packing Checklist for a Trip** – Generate a packing checklist for a [Type of Trip: beach vacation, hiking adventure, business trip] to [Destination].
- **Best Time to Visit a Destination** – When is the best time to visit [Destination], considering weather, crowds, and special events?
- **Budget Travel Tips** – Provide five budget-friendly travel tips for visiting [Destination].
- **Hotel & Accommodation Recommendations** – Recommend the best hotels in [Destination] for a [Budget/Luxury/Families/Couples] stay.
- **Cultural Etiquette & Travel Tips** – What are some essential cultural etiquette tips for travelers visiting [Destination]?
- **Solo Travel Safety Tips** – Provide safety advice for solo travelers visiting [Destination].
- **Road Trip Route Planning** – Plan a scenic road trip route from [Starting Point] to [Destination], including must-visit stops.
- **Language Survival Phrases for Travelers** – Provide ten essential phrases in [Language] for travelers visiting [Country].
- **Travel Blog Post Idea** – Generate five unique blog post ideas for a travel blog about [Destination or Travel Topic].

Marketing & Branding

- **Social Media Post Ideas for a Business** – Generate five engaging social media post ideas for a [Business Type] on [Platform: Instagram, Twitter, LinkedIn, etc.].

- **Email Marketing Campaign** – Draft an email marketing campaign promoting [Product/Service] to [Target Audience].
- **Instagram Caption Generator** – Write ten creative Instagram captions for a post featuring [Image/Topic].
- **Hashtag Strategy for Social Media** – Suggest the best hashtags to use for a [Topic/Business] on Instagram and Twitter.
- **Facebook Ad Copywriting** – Write compelling ad copy for a Facebook ad promoting [Product/Service].
- **Brand Storytelling** – Write a compelling brand story for [Company Name], highlighting its mission and values.
- **Marketing Strategy Plan** – Outline a 3-month marketing strategy plan for a new [Product/Service] launch.
- **YouTube Video Title Ideas** – Suggest ten click-worthy video titles for a YouTube channel about [Topic].
- **Product Launch Announcement** – Write a social media announcement for the launch of [Product Name].
- **Influencer Collaboration Pitch** – Draft a collaboration email for an influencer to promote [Product/Brand].
- **Sales Pitch Writing** – Write a sales pitch for this product: [Insert Product Description Here]
- **Product Description Writing** – Write a compelling product description for [Insert Product Name and Features Here]
- **SEO Optimization Tips** – Give me five tips to improve the SEO of my website
- **Product Naming Ideas** – Generate ten unique names for a new [Insert Product Type Here]
- **Slogan Generation** – Generate five catchy slogans for [Insert Brand, Product, or Event Here]

- **Podcast Topic Ideas** – Generate ten interesting podcast topic ideas for the field of [Insert Field Here]

Research & Data Analytics

- **Industry Trend Analysis** – Provide insights on the latest trends in [Industry].
- **Competitor Research Summary** – Summarize key findings from a competitor analysis for [Industry/Business].
- **Data Visualization Suggestions** – Suggest the best type of data visualization for representing [Dataset Description].
- **Statistical Analysis Explanation** – Explain the significance of [Statistical Concept] in data analysis.
- **A/B Testing Strategy** – Outline an A/B testing strategy for optimizing [Website/Marketing Campaign].
- **Customer Survey Question Design** – Create five effective survey questions to gather feedback on [Product/Service].
- **AI & Machine Learning Use Cases** – List five practical AI applications for improving [Industry or Business Process].
- **Market Research Report Summary** – Summarize key findings from a market research report on [Topic].
- **Sentiment Analysis on Social Media** – How can sentiment analysis help brands understand customer opinions on [Product/Brand]?
- **Big Data Use Cases in Finance** – How is big data transforming financial decision-making?

Business, Workflow Automation & Productivity

- **Automating Repetitive Tasks** – Suggest automation tools to streamline [Business Process].
- **Daily Workflow Optimization** – Provide a structured daily routine for maximum productivity.

- **Task Delegation Best Practices** – How should a manager effectively delegate tasks to a team?
- **CRM Automation Strategy** – Outline an automation strategy for managing customer relationships using CRM tools.
- **Meeting Agenda Template** – Provide a structured meeting agenda template for [Type of Meeting].
- **Automated Email Response Setup** – How can I set up automated email responses for [Specific Scenario]?
- **Time Tracking Tools Comparison** – Compare the top time tracking tools for freelancers.
- **Project Management Frameworks** – What are the best project management frameworks for startups?
- **AI Chatbot Integration for Customer Support** – How can AI chatbots improve customer service in [Industry]?
- **Best Practices for Remote Team Collaboration** – Provide five best practices for managing remote teams effectively.
- **Task Prioritization** – Here are my tasks for today. Help me prioritize them: [Insert Task List Here]
- **Proposal Writing** – Write a proposal for [Insert Project or Proposal Details Here]
- **Business Plan Writing** – Draft a basic business plan for a [Insert Business Type Here]
- **Creating a Study Schedule** – Help me create a study schedule for these subjects: [Insert Subject List Here]
- **Designing a Time Management Plan** – Help me design a time management plan for my weekly tasks
- **Resume Critiquing** – Critique my resume: [Insert Resume Details Here]
- **Conflict Resolution Suggestions** – Provide suggestions for resolving this conflict: [Insert Conflict Details Here]

Finance & Budgeting

- **Personal Finance Planning** – Help me create a monthly budget based on [Income and Expenses].
- **Investment Portfolio Strategy** – Suggest a diversified investment portfolio for a beginner investor.
- **Retirement Savings Plan** – How much should I save for retirement if I plan to retire at [Age]?
- **Cryptocurrency Market Trends** – What are the latest trends in the cryptocurrency market?
- **Small Business Financial Management** – What are the best financial practices for small business owners?
- **Credit Score Improvement Tips** – Provide five tips to improve a credit score quickly.
- **Tax Savings Strategies** – What are some tax-saving strategies for freelancers?
- **Cost-Cutting Measures for Businesses** – Suggest five ways a business can reduce operational costs.
- **Wealth-Building Strategies** – Outline key wealth-building strategies for young professionals.
- **Financial Risk Management** – How can companies effectively manage financial risks?
- **Budgeting Advice** – Provide advice on creating a monthly budget with these details: [Insert Financial Details Here]

Sports & Fitness

- **Custom Workout Plan** – Create a personalized 4-week fitness plan tailored for [Beginner/Intermediate/Advanced] level, focusing on [Goal: weight loss, muscle gain, endurance, flexibility]. Include a structured workout schedule, recommended exercises, rest days, and nutritional guidelines to complement the program.

- **Pre-Game Mental Preparation Tips** – Provide mental preparation strategies for athletes before a competition.
- **Sports Analytics & Performance Metrics** – How can data analytics improve performance in [Sport]?
- **Healthy Meal Plan for Athletes** – Design a meal plan for an athlete training for [Event/Sport].
- **Home Gym Setup Guide** – What equipment is essential for setting up a home gym?
- **Yoga Routine for Stress Relief** – Provide a 15-minute yoga routine for stress relief.
- **Sports Coaching Techniques** – What are the best coaching strategies for youth sports teams?
- **Hydration Strategies for Endurance Athletes** – How should endurance athletes stay hydrated during training?
- **Cycling Training Program** – Create an 8-week training program for a beginner cyclist.
- **Post-Workout Recovery Tips** – Provide five effective post-workout recovery techniques.
- **Healthy Recipe Suggestions** – Suggest a healthy recipe for dinner with these ingredients: [Insert Ingredients Here]
- **Guide for Breathing Techniques** – Provide a step-by-step guide to effective breathing techniques for [Stress Relief/Athletic Performance/Better Sleep/Meditation/Anxiety/ Reduction]. Include instructions on breath control, timing, and the physiological benefits of each technique

VISUAL STYLES IN AI: 50 PROMPTS FOR IMAGE GENERATION

Imagine being able to bring your wildest dreams to life with just a few words. That's the magic of AI-generated imagery, where your imagination is the only limit. I've put together 50 prompts designed to spark your creativity and guide AI tools to create stunning visuals.

To get started, I recommend experimenting with AI tools like Dall-e, Midjourney, and Firefly. These platforms are user-friendly and offer a wide array of customization options, allowing you to tailor your creations to your liking. You can combine elements from different prompts to create hybrid designs that blend styles and ideas. Adjusting color schemes and compositions can also dramatically alter the mood and impact of your image, giving you control over the final outcome.

Key points for crafting good AI image prompts:

Be specific: Clearly describe the subject, colors, textures, and details you want in the image.

Use artistic styles: Mention specific artists or art movements to influence the aesthetic.

Set a mood or emotion: Describe the feeling you want the image to evoke (e.g., "dreamy," "eerie," "joyful").

Consider perspective and composition: Specify the angle and framing you want for the image.

Include modifiers: Use words like "detailed," "high-resolution," "realistic," or "stylized" to refine the output.

Photorealistic (With Camera Details)

- **Golden Hour Portrait** – A young woman with curly hair illuminated by golden hour sunlight, shot with a **Canon EOS R5 + 85mm f/1.2 lens, wide aperture for dreamy bokeh**. Her freckles glow softly in the warm light.
- **Rainy Night in Tokyo** – A busy Shibuya street at night, neon lights reflecting off wet pavement. Captured with a **Sony A7R IV + 35mm f/1.4 lens, slow shutter (1/15s) to create motion blur of pedestrians**.
- **Cinematic Noir Detective Scene** – A hard-boiled detective in a dimly lit 1940s alley, cigarette smoke curling around his

face. Captured on **Leica M11 + 50mm f/2 lens, moody low-key lighting with high contrast**.

- **Macro Shot of a Butterfly on a Flower** – A vividly detailed close-up of a monarch butterfly on a dewdrop-covered flower, taken with a **Nikon D850 + 105mm f/2.8 macro lens, high detail, soft background blur**.
- **Astrophotography – Milky Way Over a Desert** – A breathtaking night sky with the Milky Way stretching over sand dunes, shot with a **Sony A7S III + 14mm f/1.8 lens, long exposure (30s), deep colors, star clarity**.
- **Black & White Portrait of a Victorian Gentleman** – A **photorealistic portrait taken with an 1890s-style large format camera, soft lighting, grainy texture**, a bearded man in a three-piece suit staring intensely into the lens.
- **Sepia-Toned 19th-Century Wild West Town** – A **sepia photograph of a dusty Western town**, a cowboy on horseback in front of a saloon, taken with an old brass lens for a vintage look.
- **Dramatic Portrait in High-Contrast Black & White** – A **portrait shot on a Leica Monochrom + 50mm f/1.4, Rembrandt lighting, sharp shadows** highlighting an old man's wrinkles.
- **Long-Exposure Waterfall in Iceland** – A breathtaking waterfall captured with a **Canon EOS R5 + 16-35mm f/2.8, long exposure (1s) for silky water effect, dramatic stormy sky**.
- **Moody Rainy Street at Night** – A misty street illuminated by a single lamplight, **shot on a Fujifilm X100V, 35mm f/2 lens, soft focus rain reflections**, a woman in a trench coat walking with an umbrella.

Surrealism & Modern Art

- **Melting Clock Cityscape** – A dreamlike city where skyscrapers and clocks melt like in a Salvador Dalí painting, with distorted perspectives and floating objects.
- **Human Head as a Glass Aquarium** – A realistic human face with an aquarium inside, filled with glowing jellyfish and floating bubbles, blending surrealism and photorealism.
- **A Giant Hand Holding a Miniature Galaxy** – A massive hyper-realistic hand floating in space, with an entire galaxy resting in its palm, stars twinkling around the fingertips.
- **Pixelated Reality – A Man Breaking into Glitch Blocks** – A person walking forward while parts of their body dissolve into pixelated data fragments, blending cyberpunk and surrealist elements.
- **Endless Escher-like Staircase** – A mysterious black-and-white world of never-ending staircases, inspired by M.C. Escher, with people walking in impossible directions.
- **A Floating Island with a Giant Tree in the Sky** – A massive ancient tree growing on a floating rock, surrounded by swirling clouds and waterfalls cascading into nothingness.
- **A Human Face Made of Butterflies** – A portrait where a person's face is dissolving into colorful, fluttering butterflies against a sunset sky.
- **A Glass City Underwater** – A futuristic city completely submerged underwater, with glowing fish swimming through transparent skyscrapers.
- **Time Collapsing – A Person Walking Through Multiple Eras** – A surreal image of a person stepping through doors leading to different time periods (prehistoric, medieval, futuristic).
- **A Spiral Galaxy Forming from a Cup of Coffee** – A hyper-

realistic coffee cup where the foam swirls into an entire galaxy, stars and planets orbiting within.

Other Styles (Modern, Impressionist, Gothic, Abstract, Low-poly 3D, Futuristic)

- **Modern Art – Geometric Portrait in Bold Colors** – A face made of geometric shapes, painted in vibrant, contrasting colors, inspired by cubism and contemporary abstract art.
- **Impressionist Style – A Riverside Picnic** – A 19th-century painting of a lively group having a picnic by the Seine, in soft brushstrokes and warm, pastel hues.
- **Gothic Fantasy Castle at Dusk** – A dark, ominous castle on a cliff, surrounded by mist and gargoyle statues, illuminated by eerie blue moonlight.
- **Low-Poly 3D Cyber City** – A futuristic city in a low-poly 3D art style, with neon-lit roads and geometric buildings, minimalistic but vibrant.
- **Abstract AI Consciousness – A Digital Neural Network Forming a Face** – A swirling mass of blue and purple digital data streams shaping into a human face, glowing with electric energy.
- **Futuristic Cyberpunk Street with Neon Signs** – A bustling urban scene with holographic billboards, rain-slicked streets reflecting neon blues and purples.
- **Impressionist Painting of a Parisian Street in the 1800s** – A soft, oil-painting-style scene of people in elegant 19th-century attire walking through a lamp-lit boulevard.
- **Low-Poly 3D Fantasy Forest** – A simplistic but beautiful low-poly forest with polygonal trees, glowing mushrooms, and a mysterious cave entrance.
- **Gothic Cathedral at Midnight with a Full Moon** – A hauntingly beautiful cathedral with towering spires, deep blue lighting, and bats flying against a giant full moon.

- **Abstract Expressionism – Chaos in Colors** – A wild, energetic abstract painting filled with splashes of bright red, yellow, and blue, conveying raw emotion.

Nature Scenes and Wild Animals

- **A Hidden Waterfall in a Misty Jungle** – A secret paradise with a crystal-clear waterfall plunging into a turquoise pool, surrounded by lush green foliage.
- **Cherry Blossom Trees in Full Bloom** – A peaceful pathway covered in pink cherry blossoms, petals floating in the air as a soft breeze moves through.
- **Aurora Borealis Over a Frozen Lake** – A stunning Arctic landscape with the Northern Lights dancing in vivid green and purple colors above an icy lake.
- **A Desert Oasis at Sunset** – A small, tranquil lagoon in the middle of golden sand dunes, palm trees reflecting in the water as the sun sets.
- **A Field of Sunflowers Under a Stormy Sky** – A dramatic contrast between bright golden sunflowers and dark, brooding storm clouds, wind bending the stalks.
- **A Majestic Snow Leopard on a Rocky Mountain Ledge** – A detailed portrait of a snow leopard, piercing blue eyes, thick winter fur, against a snowy Himalayan backdrop.
- **A Golden Eagle Soaring Over the Grand Canyon** – A powerful bird of prey mid-flight, wings spread wide, sharp focus on its talons and beak.
- **A Lush Rainforest with a Jaguar Stalking Its Prey** – A photorealistic scene of a jaguar moving silently through dense foliage, sunlight filtering through the canopy.
- **A Close-Up of a Red Fox in Autumn** – A warm, detailed close-up of a red fox with golden leaves in the background, shot with a **Canon 5D Mark IV + 135mm f/2 lens for creamy bokeh**.

- **A Humpback Whale Breaching the Ocean at Sunset** – A massive whale leaping out of the water, droplets flying everywhere, with golden light reflecting off the waves.

Anime Style

- **Cyberpunk Samurai in Neo-Tokyo** – A futuristic samurai in a neon-lit Tokyo street, wearing a high-tech armored suit, glowing katana in hand. The city is bustling with holographic signs and flying cars.
- **Magical Girl Transformation Scene** – A young girl in a sailor-style outfit surrounded by sparkling energy as she transforms into a warrior of light, with pastel pink and blue hues dominating the scene.
- **Dark Fantasy Anime Villain** – A menacing figure with piercing red eyes, dressed in flowing black robes with magical sigils. The background is a ruined castle under a blood moon.
- **Slice-of-Life Cozy Café** – A warm and inviting anime-style coffee shop with wooden furniture, sunlight streaming in, and a friendly barista serving latte art.
- **Mecha Battle in the Sky** – Two giant mechs engaging in aerial combat above a futuristic city, with laser blasts illuminating the night sky.
- **Fantasy Anime Princess in a Magical Forest** – A princess with long flowing silver hair, wearing a shimmering dress, surrounded by glowing fireflies in an enchanted, moss-covered forest.
- **High-Speed Racing Anime Scene** – A futuristic racecar speeding down a neon highway, motion blur effects, and an intense driver wearing a cyberpunk visor.
- **Post-Apocalyptic Samurai Warrior** – A lone warrior standing on a ruined city rooftop, tattered cape blowing in the wind, holding a futuristic katana.

- **Steampunk Airship Adventure** – A group of anime-style explorers on a massive floating airship, dressed in Victorian-style clothing with mechanical gadgets.
- **Festival Fireworks Over a Japanese Temple** – A young anime couple in traditional yukata watching a colorful firework display above a historic temple at night.

CONCLUSION

As we reach the end of our journey through the world of generative AI, I want to reflect on all that we've covered. From the fundamentals of AI and machine learning to the cutting-edge tools and techniques that are revolutionizing industries, this book has been a comprehensive guide to harnessing the power of AI in your everyday life.

Throughout these pages, we've focused on the practical applications of AI, showing you how to use tools like ChatGPT, Claude, Gemini, Perplexity, and Copilot to enhance your productivity and creativity. Whether you're a writer looking to overcome writer's block, an artist seeking inspiration, or a professional aiming to streamline your workflow, these AI assistants can be game-changers. We've explored their unique capabilities and provided step-by-step guidance on how to get the most out of each one.

But as you've learned, mastering AI isn't just about knowing which buttons to press. It's about understanding the art of prompt engineering—crafting the perfect input to get the desired output. We've covered the fundamentals of prompt engineering, from basic techniques to advanced strategies, and provided you with 20 essential templates to kickstart your AI interactions. By now, you should feel confident in communicating effectively with AI and leveraging its power to achieve your goals.

One of the most exciting aspects of AI is its potential to transform how we work. We've delved into the many ways AI can be integrated into professional settings, from automating routine tasks to fostering creative problem-solving. But we've also addressed the ethical considerations that come with this technology, emphasizing the importance of responsible AI development and deployment. As you embark on your AI journey, I encourage you to keep these principles in mind and strive to use AI to benefit not just yourself but society as a whole.

Of course, AI isn't just about work. It's also about play, and the possibilities for monetizing your AI skills are endless. Whether you're an entrepreneur looking to develop new products, a freelancer seeking to build a career in AI, or simply someone who wants to explore the creative potential of this technology, the strategies and examples provided in this book will set you on the right path.

As we look to the future, one thing is clear: AI is here to stay, and it will only become more prevalent in our lives. By staying informed about the latest trends and advancements, and committing to lifelong learning, you'll be well-positioned to ride the wave of AI innovation. The bonus sections, recommended tools, and learning resources included in this book are designed to help you do just that, providing a roadmap for continued growth and exploration.

But knowledge alone isn't enough. To truly reap the benefits of AI, you need to take action. I challenge you to start experimenting with the tools and techniques you've learned, engage with the vibrant AI community, and pursue projects pushing the boundaries of what's possible. Whether you're building your own personal AI assistant, developing a new product, or simply exploring the creative potential of this technology, every small step you take brings you closer to mastering the art of AI.

As I conclude this book, I want to express my gratitude for your commitment to learning about this transformative technology. It's been a pleasure to share my knowledge and passion with you, and I hope this book has informed you and inspired you to embrace the power of AI in your own life. Remember, the journey doesn't end here. Keep learning, keep experimenting, and keep pushing yourself to new heights. If you found value in this book, I'd be grateful if you could take a moment to leave a review on Amazon so that others can also benefit from this resource.

The future of AI is bright, and I'm excited to see where your AI journey takes you. Whether you're a beginner just starting out or a seasoned pro looking to take your skills to the next level, always remember that anything is possible with the right tools, techniques, and mindset. So go forth, my friend, and embrace the power of AI. The world is waiting for you to make your mark.

KEEPING THE GAME ALIVE

Now that you've got **everything you need to start using AI to 10x your productivity, boost creativity, and make everyday life easier**, it's time to **pay it forward** and help others get started too.

Here's how you can do that:

Leave an honest review of this book on Amazon.

Your review helps **other curious beginners** — just like you — find the same tools, tips, and inspiration you've discovered. You'll be **showing them where to start** and giving them the confidence to jump into this amazing world of AI.

Thank you so much for helping out.

AI isn't just about machines — it's about **people helping people**.

When we share what we've learned, **we keep the AI revolution alive and growing** — and **you're now a part of that story**.

Click here to leave your review on Amazon.

Thanks again — and here's to using AI to make life better, one smart move at a time!

— Kai Sinclair

REFERENCES

- *Timeline of artificial intelligence* https://en.wikipedia.org/wiki/Timeline_of_artificial_intelligence
- *Narrow AI vs General AI* https://www.geeksforgeeks.org/narrow-ai-vs-general-ai/
- *Why Data Matters in the AI Revolution* https://www.akkio.com/post/importance-of-data-in-ai
- *A Beginner's Guide to Neural Networks and Deep Learning* https://wiki.pathmind.com/neural-network
- *How to use ChatGPT for customer service* https://www.techtarget.com/searchcustomerexperience/feature/How-to-use-ChatGPT-for-customer-service
- *Using Google Gemini to Write a Screenplay | by Leon Nicholls* https://leonnicholls.medium.com/using-google-gemini-to-write-a-screenplay-5771614ccee8
- *Introducing the analysis tool in Claude.ai* https://www.anthropic.com/news/analysis-tool
- *How to Use Midjourney: A Comprehensive Guide to AI ...* https://www.datacamp.com/tutorial/how-to-use-midjourney-a-comprehensive-guide-to-ai-generated-artwork-creation
- *Prompt Engineering Guide* https://www.promptingguide.ai/
- *ChatGPT vs. Google Bard vs. Bing Chat vs. Claude* https://searchengineland.com/chatgpt-google-bard-bing-chat-claude-best-generative-ai-solution-436888
- *6 advanced AI prompt engineering techniques for better outputs* https://outshift.cisco.com/blog/advanced-ai-prompt-engineering-techniques
- *How to Write Good AI Prompts: A Beginner's Guide (+12 ...* https://www.getmagical.com/blog/how-to-write-good-ai-prompts
- *How to Make an AI Assistant in 10 Steps* https://litslink.com/blog/create-ai-assistant
- *Leading AI Platforms of 2023: A Compilation of the Best 12* https://www.linkedin.com/pulse/leading-ai-platforms-2023-compilation-best-12-paresh-patil-05qrf
- *How AI Tools Are Revolutionizing Google Calendar* https://www.getclockwise.com/blog/ai-tool-google-calendar
- *Document AI* https://cloud.google.com/document-ai

- *AI-Powered Tools Transforming Task Management and ...* https://www.topbots.com/ai-tools-task-management-scheduling/
- *How AI Can Transform Creative Problem-Solving and ...* https://medium.com/aimonks/how-ai-can-transform-creative-problem-solving-and-innovation-within-teams-ba0838ba1f09
- *15 Must-Have AI Tools for Remote Team Collaboration* https://www.goprofiles.io/blog/15-ai-tools-for-remote-team-collaboration/
- *Five Ethical Issues of AI in the Modern Workplace - SDI* https://www.servicedeskinstitute.com/resources/five-ethical-issues-of-ai-in-the-modern-workplace/
- *10 Business Models That Reimagine The Value Creation ...* https://www.forbes.com/councils/forbestechcouncil/2021/05/05/10-business-models-that-reimagine-the-value-creation-of-ai-and-ml/
- *AI for E-commerce and Customer Experience* https://blog.evolv.ai/ai-for-ecommerce-and-cx
- *Find & Hire AI engineers: 15 Best Sites [2025]* https://www.developersforhire.com/ai
- *How AI Can Affect Intellectual Property And What It Means ...* https://www.forbes.com/councils/forbesbusinesscouncil/2024/08/20/how-ai-can-affect-intellectual-property-and-what-it-means-for-leaders/
- *AI and IoT Collaboration in Addressing Industry Challenges* https://www.veritis.com/blog/ai-and-iot-collaboration-in-addressing-industry-challenges/
- *The state of AI in 2023: Generative AI's breakout year* https://www.mckinsey.com/capabilities/quantumblack/our-insights/the-state-of-ai-in-2023-generative-ais-breakout-year
- *Artificial intelligence in healthcare: transforming the ...* https://pmc.ncbi.nlm.nih.gov/articles/PMC8285156/
- *A Practical Guide to Building Ethical AI* https://hbr.org/2020/10/a-practical-guide-to-building-ethical-ai
- *40 Best ChatGPT Prompts For Productivity (Boost ... - Weam AI* https://weam.ai/blog/prompts/best-chatgpt-prompts-for-productivity/
- *Choosing the Best AI Image Generator Technology of 2023* https://snapbar.com/blog/deciphering-ai-image-generator-technology-of-2023
- *AI Tools for Beginners: A Comprehensive Guide* https://medium.com/@fahmiadam/ai-tools-for-beginners-a-comprehensive-guide-0c71f4416d73
- *AI for Beginners* https://microsoft.github.io/AI-For-Beginners/
- [1] RedRess Compliance. (n.d.). Microsoft Copilot integration: Top 10 software integrations. https://redresscompliance.com/microsoft-copilot-integration-top10-software-integrations/

- [2] WPS.ai. (n.d.). How to use Copilot Pro in Microsoft Word/Excel/PowerPoint. https://www.wps.ai/blog/how-to-use-copilot-pro-in-microsoft-word-excel-powerpoint/
- [3] Axon. (n.d.). How to implement Microsoft Copilot into your application. https://www.axon.dev/blog/how-to-implement-microsoft-copilot-into-your-application
- Arizona State University. (n.d.). Microsoft 365 Copilot. https://ai.asu.edu/microsoft-365-copilot
- Nadella, S. (2023, March 16). Introducing Microsoft 365 Copilot: Your Copilot for work. Microsoft Blog. https://blogs.microsoft.com/blog/2023/03/16/introducing-microsoft-365-copilot-your-copilot-for-work/
- SHI. (n.d.). How to use Copilot in Microsoft Teams, Word, Excel and more. https://blog.shi.com/business-of-it/how-to-use-copilot-in-microsoft-teams-word-excel-and-more/
- Microsoft. (n.d.). Microsoft 365 Copilot requirements. https://learn.microsoft.com/th-th/copilot/microsoft-365/microsoft-365-copilot-requirements
- Microsoft. (n.d.). How to use Copilot in Microsoft Teams, Word, Excel and more [Video]. YouTube. https://www.youtube.com/watch?v=tIpCe1snCHo
- Creighton University Libraries. (n.d.). Perplexity AI. https://culibraries.creighton.edu/c.php?g=1334271&p=10213131
- Kuka, V. (n.d.). 14 Perplexity AI use cases: The search engine you didn't know could do so much. Learn Prompting. https://learnprompting.org/blog/perplexity_use_cases
- OpenTools.ai. (n.d.). Perplexity AI unveils multimodal mobile assistant exclusively for Android. https://opentools.ai/news/perplexity-ai-unveils-multimodal-mobile-assistant-exclusively-for-android
- Reddit. (2024). What are some use cases for Perplexity AI? r/perplexity_ai. https://www.reddit.com/r/perplexity_ai/comments/1dmcf20/what_are_some_use_cases_for_perplexity_ai/
- YouTube. (n.d.). [Video title not provided]. https://www.youtube.com/watch?v=lWBtWk0JZrc
- Benzinga. (2024, January 25). Perplexity debuts AI-powered mobile assistant on Android, rivals Google with multimodal features, but there are some gaps. https://www.benzinga.com/25/01/43186357/perplexity-debuts-ai-powered-mobile-assistant-on-android-rivals-google-with-multimodal-features-but-there-are-some-gaps
- Elegant Themes. (n.d.). Perplexity AI. https://www.elegantthemes.com/blog/business/perplexity-ai
- Reddit. (2024). Real time web search. r/perplexity_ai. https://www.reddit.com/r/perplexity_ai/comments/1f251sf/real_time_web_search/

- TechTarget. (n.d.). How to use Perplexity AI: Tutorial, pros and cons. https://www.techtarget.com/searchenterpriseai/tutorial/How-to-use-Perplexity-AI-Tutorial-pros-and-cons
- Ohio Society of Association Professionals. (n.d.). [Article title not provided]. https://www.ohiosap.org/aws/OSAP/pt/sd/news_article/577041/_blank/layout_details/false
- Photon Insights. (n.d.). Perplexity AI. https://www.photoninsights.com/blog/perplexity-ai/
- Cointelegraph. (2024, January 7). ChatGPT vs. Grok AI: What's the difference? https://cointelegraph.com/learn/articles/chatgpt-vs-grok-ai-differences
- Deep Water Management. (2024, July 5). AI Benchmarking: Evaluating Model Performance on Subjective, Complex, and Predictive Queries. https://deepwatermgmt.com/ai-benchmarking-evaluating-model-performance-on-subjective-complex-and-predictive-queries/
- EM360. (2024, December 9). Is xAI's Grok Better than ChatGPT? A Comparison. https://em360tech.com/tech-articles/xais-grok-better-chatgpt-comparison
- Julius AI. (2024, May 11). Comparing Grok AI to ChatGPT. https://julius.ai/articles/comparing-grok-ai-to-chatgpt
- Reddit. (2024, November 27). How does Grok compare to chatGPT? [Reddit post]. r/OpenAI. https://www.reddit.com/r/OpenAI/comments/1h0x4yv/how_does_grok_compare_to_chatgpt/
- TechRadar. (2024, December 30). Grok vs. ChatGPT: Can Elon Musk's X take on AI giant OpenAI? https://www.techradar.com/pro/grok-vs-chatgpt-can-elon-musks-x-take-on-ai-giant-openai
- CNBC. (2025, January 30). DeepSeek's AI claims have shaken the world — but not everyone's convinced. https://www.cnbc.com/2025/01/30/chinas-deepseek-has-some-big-ai-claims-not-all-experts-are-convinced-.html
- IBM. (2025, January 27). DeepSeek's reasoning AI shows power of small models, efficiently trained. https://www.ibm.com/think/news/deepseek-r1-ai
- KPMG. (2025, January 29). DeepSeek: A breakthrough moment for AI. https://kpmg.com/us/en/media/news/insights-on-deepseek.html
- CloudFabrix. (2025, January 30). DeepSeek: Revolutionizing AI Development Through Cost-Effective Innovation. https://cloudfabrix.com/blog/deepseek-revolutionizing-ai-development-through-cost-effective-innovation/
- The Register. (2025, January 26). China's DeepSeek just dropped a free challenger to OpenAI's o1 – here's how to use it on your PC. https://www.theregister.com/2025/01/26/deepseek_r1_ai_cot/

- Yahoo News. (2025, January 31). Research exposes DeepSeek's AI training cost is not $6M, it's a staggering $1.3B. https://www.yahoo.com/news/research-exposes-deepseek-ai-training-165025904.html
- Encord. (2024, November 4). OpenAI's DALL-E 3 explained: Generate images with ChatGPT. https://encord.com/blog/openai-dall-e-3-what-we-know-so-far/
- MIT Sloan Education Technology. (2023, October 20). Timely insights & use cases for OpenAI in the classroom: DALL-E imagery and ChatGPT's image analysis. https://mitsloanedtech.mit.edu/2023/10/20/timely-insights-use-cases-for-openai-in-the-classroom-dalle-imagery-and-chatgpts-image-analysis-voice-functionality/
- OpenAI. (n.d.). Improving image generation with better captions [PDF]. https://cdn.openai.com/papers/dall-e-3.pdf
- WhyTryAI. (2023, November 2). The secret sauce behind DALL-E 3: How is it so great at following prompts? https://www.whytryai.com/p/dall-e-3-better-captions-research-paper-summary
- Adobe. (n.d.). Adobe Firefly overview. https://helpx.adobe.com/firefly/get-set-up/learn-the-basics/adobe-firefly-overview.html
- VentureBeat. (2024). Adobe launches Firefly 3 with full AI image generation in Photoshop. https://venturebeat.com/ai/adobe-launches-firefly-3-with-full-ai-image-generation-in-photoshop/
- Adobe. (2024, October 14). Adobe launches Firefly video model. https://news.adobe.com/news/2024/10/101424-adobe-launches-firefly-video-model
- Creative Bloq. (n.d.). Everything you need to know about Adobe Firefly. https://www.creativebloq.com/features/everything-you-need-to-know-about-adobe-firefly
- CreativePro. (2025). What's new in Adobe Creative Cloud 2025. https://creativepro.com/whats-new-in-adobe-creative-cloud-2025/
- Adobe. (2024). What's new in Adobe Firefly. https://helpx.adobe.com/firefly/using/whats-new/2024.html
- Adobe. (n.d.). What's new in Adobe Firefly. https://helpx.adobe.com/firefly/whats-new/new-features/whats-new.html
- Adobe. (2024). Adobe introduces Firefly Image 3 foundation model to take creative exploration and ideation to new heights. https://news.adobe.com/news/news-details/2024/adobe-introduces-firefly-image-3-foundation-model-to-take-creative-exploration-and-ideation-to-new-heights
- PPM Express. (2025). *10 best AI project management tools in 2025*. Retrieved February 11, 2025, from https://ppm.express/blog/10-best-ai-project-management-tools-in-2025/

- TrackingTime. (2024). *Asana vs Monday vs ClickUp: In-depth project management software showdown*. Retrieved February 11, 2025, from https://trackingtime.co/best-practices/asana-vs-monday-vs-clickup-in-depth-project-management-software-showdown.html
- StackShare. (n.d.). MindMeister vs XMind: What are the differences? https://stackshare.io/stackups/mindmeister-vs-xmind
- Research Studies Press. (2024, April 15). The role of artificial intelligence in smart cities: Enhancing urban living. https://research-studies-press.co.uk/2024/04/15/the-role-of-artificial-intelligence-in-smart-cities-enhancing-urban-living-2/
- United States Artificial Intelligence Institute. (n.d.). Certified Artificial Intelligence Consultant (CAIC™). https://www.usaii.org/artificial-intelligence-certifications/certified-artificial-intelligence-consultant?utm_source=chatgpt.com
- CertNexus. (n.d.). Certified Artificial Intelligence Practitioner (CAIP). https://certnexus.com/certified-artificial-intelligence-practitioner-caip/?utm_source=chatgpt.com
- Marr, B. (2025, January 20). Why agentic AI will soon make ChatGPT look like a simple calculator. *Forbes.* https://www.forbes.com/sites/bernardmarr/2025/01/20/why-agentic-ai-will-soon-make-chatgpt-look-like-a-simple-calculator/
- Rebelo, M. (2024, July 23). *The 8 best AI scheduling assistants.* Zapier. https://zapier.com/blog/best-ai-scheduling/

www.ingramcontent.com/pod-product-compliance
Lightning Source LLC
LaVergne TN
LVHW022051200926
848481LV00003B/869
9798349383472